* the toddler café *

* the toddler café *

*fast, healthy, and fun ways to feed even
the pickiest eater*

by jennifer carden * **photographs by** matthew carden

dedication ∗ *to diana b. torrey,*
for teaching me how to make even messy
food look pretty — you are missed.

Text copyright © 2008
by Jennifer Carden

Photographs copyright ©
2008 by Matthew Carden

Library of Congress
Cataloging-in-Publication
Data available.

ISBN: 978-0-8118-5927-1

Manufactured in China.

prop styling by
Jennifer Carden

food styling by
Jennifer Carden

designed by
Lesley Feldman

typesetting by
Lesley Feldman

10 9 8 7 6 5 4 3 2 1

chronicle books llc
680 Second Street
San Francisco, California
94107

www.chroniclebooks.com

acknowledgments

jennifer and *matthew* wish to thank the following people:

- *claire*, our little bean, you are the most honest recipe taster and a star for putting up with our crazy ideas and recipes. It has been so much fun watching you growing, learning, and "playing" as you explore the world of food. You are our inspiration.

- A BIG thank you to our amazing mess-makers and their parents. You all made this so much fun: *ari mcdonald, claire carden, gage rizzo, maya budwig, lily warwick, max koebel, maxine asmussen, melia chendo, oliver arnesson, sean escobar, sloan takeuchi-ross,* and *kimbrae the dog.*

- *ty, sarah,* and *imani jade,* for believing in us, inspiring us, and setting a wonderful example for our life.

- *caroll, michael, michelle, hernan,* and *briana,* thank you for all your support and love.

- To the amazing group of creative professionals at Chronicle Books—art director *brooke johnson,* production coordinator *ben kasman,* copy editor *ann rolke,* managing editors *peggy gannon* and *jennifer sparkman,* marketing manager *peter perez,* and publicists *amy portello and andrea burnett*—you have made this experience so enjoyable for us, and we truly appreciate you turning our vision into reality. And, most importantly, thanks to our project editor, *amy treadwell,* for your sense of humor and willingness to take us under your wing. Thanks to *leslie feldman* for designing this beautiful book.

jennifer wishes to thank the following people:

- Thank you to my amazing husband, *matthew,* for being my partner in everything, for dreaming up a recipe for our life with me and continually reminding me to keep it simple. Thank you for your photographs—you are always pushing the envelope with your silly and beautiful ideas. Thank you for being calm when you knew how much work I had to do and how many photos you had to edit. We decided we were going to make books when we were on "that island," and here we are making books!

- *nicole*—my amazing agent—a big thanks to you. Without you, this book might still be a scribble in my notebook.

- *mom,* for giving me culinary inspiration—you are a great cook. Thank you for giving me amazing memories of making chocolate chip cookies together.

- *dad,* for giving me advice like "Talk to everyone, you never know how it could change your life". . . and I do, and it has.

- Also thank you to both of my parents for always supporting and believing in my creative endeavors.

- *hal* and *gaila,* for always pushing my culinary knowledge with questions like "We have this deer . . ."

- *marcus* and *lori,* for blazing the trail as authors and always being there to give advice when I need it, all while shuttling around your crew, *alex, zachary, jacob, brett,* and *dylan.*

- *mrs. hillins,* for always having skirt steaks cooking in the broiler for me when I got home from school and taking such good care of me.

- I thank the following inspiring women for encouraging and believing in me, and my terrific community of friends and family for all your support and enthusiasm:

- *julie koebel,* for years of support and for keeping me on my toes with all those cooking questions; and *michelle stern,* for teaching me how to be a go-getter and giving me good laughs. You both have encouraged me from the beginning, without falter—for this I give you my deepest thanks.

- *avry mar,* for lighting the fire under me by inspiring this book and always telling me the truth.

- *the f.m. women, tamela fish, amanda arnesson,* and all my *marin moms* who cheered me on.

- *kimberly rider,* for telling me I could do it when I thought I couldn't, inspiring me to move forward, and hooking me up!

- *barbra rosenfeld,* for lending an ear and encouraging me. It seems like such a long time ago we were making hamburgers in our dorm room closet!

- *diane franey,* for taking such good care of Claire while I was working.

contents

* introduction *

don't compromise, get creative * **our world today is moving fast, and we're caught in the dragnet of convenience. the pull toward boxed macaroni and cheese is strong, and fast "foods" are everywhere. it seems so easy just to "drive thru," especially when you know your child will eat it, while you may know in the back (or the front) of your mind that this is not the best way to feed your kids. but what this teaches them is to be unconscious, unhealthy consumers of food, and it never gives them a chance to develop their palate, an interest in food, or experience natural flavors and freshness.**

Break free of the net and don't fret, there is another way—it's fun, it's fast, and just a little creative thinking can change the way your kids eat. Summon up your inner artist with these quick, fun ways to develop a toddler's interest in food and keep them at the table. Improve the meal experience for you *and* your kids with just an added dollop of creativity.

This cookbook is a springboard for you to learn how to be creative and interact with your children in a way that works best for you and them. This quick and dirty approach, with an emphasis on "dirty," will help you set up your kids' positive relationship with food for life. Love it, live it, eat it, full speed ahead!

food & family

the family that eats together eats better

The short time in a child's life between two and five years old is when they grow from having no opinions to having lots of opinions, and it's your job to give them direction. This book is about how parents can teach children to approach eating by making mealtime fun and interactive. This learning will continue to grow, setting them up to have a great relationship with food for the rest of their lives. Remember, all kids are different: this approach may not work for some children.

Family-style meals are sacred and fleeting—a nearly lost art these days. We are moving so fast from task to task and wondering why our kids can't focus and connect. Mealtimes are the perfect place to start. Sit down with your family as often as you can. If you have fragmented schedules, try to set one or two nights a week for family meals on a consistent basis. It can be difficult for families to eat together every night, but it's worth trying at least one because consistency simplifies mealtimes. Don't be afraid to let your children taste all foods: smoked, pickled, sour, bitter, and unusual flavors. The more they are exposed to the larger range of foods, the more they will learn to love food as they grow.

Then you can move on to the next step—cooking with your kids—and someday you'll achieve the ultimate goal of them cooking and eating great healthy food.

the apple doesn't fall far...

I remember cooking with my mom when I was very young, standing on a chair in our olive drab– and mustard–colored kitchen. She was never thrown off by a recipe or afraid to substitute ingredients; we just tossed in whatever we thought would taste good. Oh, and measuring wasn't something she did, either. She just had that intuition. I learned from her how the puzzle pieces of ingredients go together when creating a dish. Now my daughter is standing on a chair in our kitchen, and we are making memories and chocolate chip cookies together.

These are my memories; they revolve around food and cooking, and I want to translate these memories and experience for the next generation. As a trained chef and artist, I have gained a true understanding of how to work with ingredients creatively. When I became a mom myself, my relationship to food quickly changed. The realization that my husband and I had to literally teach someone how to eat led us to develop this approach for feeding toddlers.

My phone rings at least once a day with cooking questions from friends and family. I have always loved to help people cook and offer them new ideas. I love the challenge of cooking with just what is in the refrigerator and thinking on my feet. I see it as a challenge, but seeing how some other moms weren't feeling as creative in the kitchen as I was, I decided to embark on this project with help from my husband.

At first, we just did what we knew—being silly and thinking of kid-friendly ways to get the food into the mouth. Making cute and complicated food wasn't what worked here, though; it was the child-parent relationship that worked. It was picking up a piece of lettuce and pretending it was a bird that entertained our child and enticed her to eat! Soon our daughter was eating a wide range of foods, and we were no longer struggling with dinner table drama.

the power struggle: make fun, not war

One of the first places a child may test their control is with food. This is where the power struggle can start. Alice Sterling Honig, professor of child development at Syracuse University, says that parents usually direct and guide their toddlers in one of two ways: Power Control or Reasoning with Control.

Power Control includes physical and verbal force and withholding things such as toys and affection, while Reasoning with Control works by telling the child why he or she should act a certain way, using simple words they can understand. The studies Professor Honig reviewed showed that parents who used reasoning were better able to influence their children's behavior and teach them to cooperate.

So, be ready to accept refusal of some foods, but don't let it faze you, and don't take it personally. Be patient and creative, and you will be able to keep the situation in check. This is where the Reasoning with Control can be handy: No matter how annoyed you are, the situation will only get worse if you elevate your voice. Give praise for small steps, but try not to dilute the effect of praise by dispensing it at every little action.

If you want your child to try a new food, be casual about it. Get some for yourself as a snack, not at mealtime. Ask them if they want a taste of "X" (think up a cute or magical name) and give them a tiny taste. If they reject it, just forget about it for that moment; don't make faces or make a big deal out of it. Try serving it another time *without* saying, "This is that stuff you tasted and hated," or, "You didn't like that last time." If you say "ick," they'll say "ick." So don't say it! Your child will not eat if you won't eat. Give positive responses to ANY food you try, even if you don't love it. Just remember: You spend your days with a little sponge. They soak up everything you do. They want to be just like you, and if you won't touch it, they won't touch it.

Sometimes refusal can be turned around just by changing the temperature of the food. Some children prefer cold to warm or vice versa. Try both when introducing a new food—you may be surprised.

you are the boss

Don't make a habit of asking your child what she wants for dinner; doing so is setting a trap for yourself. Remember, you're the boss! Choices are helpful sometimes, but don't allow too many, or the situation could spiral downward quickly. Two to three choices on the plate will help a child feel like he has some power, but will still give you the upper hand by allowing you to offer what you want. Giving choices works best when your child understands that she must eat what she chooses from the plate. When you serve your child, serve the portion you expect them to eat. If it is a new food, put a very small amount on the plate. For older kids, give them a goal amount to eat, such as half or five bites, so they understand exactly what you want them to do. For more picky eaters, feed your child in stages, serving one thing to get her interest piqued, and then bringing out the next item. Kids have little stomachs and don't need as much food as we think they do. Serve small amounts, and don't overwhelm them with large portions or a plate full of too many different items. It can take up to fifteen tries of serving a new food before a toddler becomes interested, so don't be discouraged. You may be amazed by when and where they decide to try a new food and then ask for more. Once that happens, you have ammo. At the next meal you can say, "Remember when you tried 'X' and you liked it a lot?"

My daughter would not touch tuna salad with a ten-foot fairy wand until she saw my husband having some and he told her it was what mermaids liked to snack on. Then she gobbled it up like a hungry little mermaid. Kids love fantasy, so play on that— the more absurd the better.

meal routine

How your child comes to the table is usually a huge factor in what direction the meal will take. A positive mood and happy toddler will make the eating experience more enjoyable for everyone. Change and toddlers don't mix. Kids crave routine and need to know what to expect. Usually they are playing just before dinnertime and can be jolted by the call to the table; there may be resistance. Give them fair warning when the meal will be happening; for example, "When the timer goes off, see how fast you can get to the table." If time increments don't work, create your own dinner bell by hitting a soup pot with a wooden spoon— three times means dinnertime! The time will not mean anything to them, but they will definitely know it is coming. Create a fun

dinnertime routine to help avoid the throw-down tantrum that can come on so swiftly. Here are some ideas to help you get started with a new routine:

- ⬎ *Eat at the same time every night when possible.*

- ⬎ *Have your child participate in setting the table with placemats and napkins, which are manageable for small hands.*

- ⬎ *Talk about the yummy food you are going to have.*

- ⬎ *Include them in the preparation of the meal.*

- ⬎ *Don't rush; children are more likely to eat in a relaxed environment.*

- ⬎ *Start traditions such as taking turns saying one fun thing you did during the day, or something you are grateful for. Friday nights are a great night for this ritual, as it seals the week and shows a definitive start to the weekend.*

↘ *If it is just you and your child or children eating, don't leave them alone at the table to get the dishes done. Sit with them. Let them know that they are important and you can take the time to be with them. By sitting with them, you have a much better chance of encouraging them to eat with you while being interactive and creative.*

↘ *Have your child help with cleanup. This is a perfect time to teach responsibility. (See Cleanup Tips, page 14.)*

kids are messy people, too: if you can't beat 'em, join 'em

Wiping, wiping . . . that is all we were doing when our daughter was first eating, keeping her neat and tidy, not letting her clothing get those pesky carrot stains on them. One hot summer day, my good friend noticed my two-year-old very neatly eating a Popsicle, without a drip. We were so proud! But without reservation, my friend said, "Hey, let the kid have some fun, would ya? How will she ever experience anything?" That really opened our eyes and made us think about what we were doing. After a discussion with my husband where we wondered if we were permanently damaging our child's psyche, we decided to take a different approach and let her start experiencing the world of food more intimately—mostly with her hands! This is where the concept for this book was born: we would let her have the tactile experience on her own without too much interference from us, and her tastes would be her own.

Yes, feeding toddlers is messy business, so be prepared, roll up your sleeves, and jump in! You have spent the last year spoon-feeding them, and now it is time to hand over the spoon and stand back—way back. They're discovering a world of new tastes, and you have the pleasure of walking down the road with them, toting a sponge.

Don't stress the mess. It is going to happen—remember the days of baby food in the hair? Hopefully those days are over. New ways of being messy are emerging every day, and your kid is on top of it! Make sure to give positive attention to eating and less attention to mess to make the child comfortable. Try, "Please take your drumstick out of your juice. Does it taste good? Maybe we can make a recipe using juice. That is a good idea." Be positive.

Say, "Oh, what a mess! Now let's clean it up." Let your child know that making a mess is OK but that there are boundaries. Dropping food on the floor to see what happens is not OK, but dripping off the spoon by accident is just natural. You will be surprised—as they get more interested in the food, the mess will lessen. Just figure that the cleanup is part of the meal. When a child is involved in the whole process, including cleanup, it instills ownership and pride. This is an opportunity to give your child a lesson in how to be responsible for themselves.

You have to feed them, so why not have fun doing it? Get kids involved, and don't be afraid of the mess. As their ship sets sail toward the world of food, they want to be the captain. You will have to choose your battles wisely, and keeping your child spotless is a losing one, so let's try changing the course.

cleanup tips: make 'em work for you, not against you

- ❯ Teach your child how to clear their plate from the table at an early age, even if you have to remove some items to make it easier to handle.

- ❯ Get a handheld vacuum. This will be your most valuable tool. Teach your child to use this when they are ready. It is a tool they will want to use.

- ❯ Black beans harden up like cement on a toddler's face, so keep a damp, warm washcloth handy for cleanup after meals like this.

- ❯ Make for easy cleanup by using a washable and waterproof splat mat under your child's chair so you can be worry-free.

- ❯ Eat outside whenever possible.

- ❯ Use a washable high-chair cover, such as the Messeez brand.

- ❯ Make a game out of it: Use a paper cup to flick peas into under the table after dinner.

- ❯ Time to get a dog! There are some things your vacuum can't pick up that a dog would clean up happily.

- ❯ After a meal of spaghetti, give your child a cup and ask them to go on a worm hunt to clean up the escaped worms.

- ❯ Get a mini dustpan and have your child decorate it. Keep it in a special place that they can reach.

- ❯ Make a deck of oversized flash cards with different cleanup jobs on them. Each night, have your child pick one before the meal.

- ❯ Teach your child to help with the dishes. Do dishes during the day when you need an activity, and then let them help with the dishes one night a week after dinner.

- ❯ Throw on a bib.

- ❯ Use wipes sparingly; they usually have a strong scent that can be unappetizing during a meal. They are also not great for the environment; a washcloth can do the same job.

- ❯ A bath is always a good idea—go straight from table to tub!

walking the fine line: manners vs. fun

I'm not saying to give your child permission to go crazy at the dinner table; you have to set boundaries and enforce them, but try to let them enjoy meals, too. Be consistent; don't let them bend the rules one day and not another day. Here are some suggestions that may help you create a calm and enjoyable mealtime.

> *No toys at the table. Toys can be very distracting, and taking them away can create a power struggle. (Exception to the rule: Inviting stuffed animals to dinner. They get seats away from the child's reach.)*

> *Basic manners: "Please," "Thank you," and "No, thank you" to start. Add more as you feel appropriate.*

> *Making a mess by accident is OK; trying to make a mess is not.*

> *No playing with silverware; forks and spoons are not toys. Respect the tools.*

You can gently enforce behavior by saying, for example, "We only use our forks for eating, not for combing the dog," or "We can brush the dog after dinner. Would you like to do that?" If you escalate your mood and get angry or draw a lot of attention to misbehavior, your child will probably exaggerate the offending action.

home cooking: wow, it smells so good!

What makes a home-cooked meal better than a pre-prepared one? Prepared food certainly can have a place in our busy lives, occasionally. But prepared foods can be full of sodium and fats used to extend shelf life. Avoiding chemical preservatives and unhealthy fats is another great reason to cook at home. Cooking at home is cost-effective, too; make enough for leftovers to eat for lunch the next day. Or, make a double recipe to freeze and eat next week when you are in a time pinch.

Walking in the door after a long day of playing or school to be met with the comforting smell of food can be one of the best memories for a child, but it doesn't have to be complicated for you. We remember with all of our senses, and smell can be a huge part of a child's memory. Cooking at home is so wonderful because it promotes family interaction—something we are losing in our society at an alarming rate. Inviting your kids into the kitchen to help can be a great interactive learning activity, since as parents, we are our children's teachers. Spending time together while promoting healthy choices is a perfect way to end a day.

creativity is confidence

Let your inner artist come out! Discover your creativity and don't waste time on complicated recipes.

All of the recipes in this book are based on the idea that you can make great meals from what you have on hand. Being creative in the kitchen may not seem like your thing, but when you gain confidence with ingredients, tools, and new tastes, meals will get easier and easier. Experiment and have fun, but remember that you are cooking for youngsters! This is an exploration for both you and your child. Let them get to know how food feels, smells, and tastes. Yes, I said "feels!" Some children are more comfortable using their sense of touch in addition to smell and sight, so just go with it.

Toddlers are picky little creatures, and something that was beloved yesterday may be feared like the plague today. Spending hours on a meal just to have it rejected is not what you're after. You can introduce new foods and flavors in simple and quick ways.

In this new way of looking at food, you can create quick, interactive dishes for kids that get them interested in what is on the plate without sacrificing your own dinnertime enjoyment. This is where you have to muster up your creative spirit—be as silly as you can, and your child will focus on you and probably eat the food without a struggle. Occasionally, when all else fails, you might have to resort to the DSM (Distract and Shovel Method), but hopefully you won't have to go there too often.

Get them used to seeing different foods arrive on the table each night. Try to have a bunch of sauces and spices on the table so everyone can tailor their meal to their liking. As your child sees you pouring on the different sauces, they will want to try, too. If they want to put Asian plum sauce on their spaghetti, let them —they may like it! Make sure you explain what the flavor tastes like, though; if they don't know what is coming and taste a hot or spicy sauce, it can backfire. Let them try what they are interested in; if it is spicy or strong, make sure you have some cooling milk standing by, because water doesn't help "'picy!"

Get your kids used to tasting herbs and spices by letting them gently smell the jars or fresh herbs when you are in the kitchen. Turn it into a fun guessing game such as "Smell the Spices," making sure not to let them sniff so hard or so close that they get spices up their noses. Keep the too-spicy ones out of reach.

Each time you make these recipes, try adding a new flavor. Try a different cooking technique or serve it up differently, and you will train your kids to get excited about a variety of foods as you expand the whole family's confidence about food. You can do it!

setting the stage: plating, shapes, and styling

Some of the creative fun can be started in the kitchen before you bring the food to the table. Here are some ideas to get you started.

- **design a meal** * *Cut foods in strips and arrange them in patterns on the plate, making up a story about the "house or sticks on the forest floor."*

- **color course** * *Bring out one food at a time, by color. "Here comes green . . . ," and "Here comes white . . ."*

- **mounds and mounds** * *Make mounds out of spinach, potatoes, or eggs, for something different.*

- **cut it up** * *Cut out shapes of bread, cheese, and polenta with cookie cutters.*

- **hide-a-veggie** * *Stick peas inside a few pieces of penne pasta and have them search for the "gem."*

- **brown bag it** * *Serve food such as dry cereal or crackers in paper cones made from brown bags and tape.*

- **birds in motion** * *Chop romaine lettuce leaves in strips across the middle rib to look like birds.*

- **wrap it up** * *Wrap foods such as vegetables and bread in aluminum foil and have them unwrap it at the table.*

- **fork lift** * *Place veggies or food in a decorative pattern on the tines of the fork to get them started and interested.*

- **big magnet** * *Give your child a plain cooked noodle and have them dip it into shredded nori or nuts or coconut, and "magically" the pasta will pick up the food.*

creative food play

Getting your child's imagination going can be one of the best ways to raise their interest in eating. Use these techniques for creative food play when you get stuck in a rut, or just to spice up the fun at meals. For food play, use metaphors instead of games. If you do invent games at the table, try not to make the games so distracting that the child's focus is led away from the task of eating. The most important thing is, remember to be silly—like a kid would be—and let loose.

Here are some fun ways to get their imagination going at the table. Check out the recipes for more ideas.

↘ **animal association** * *When trying to get them to eat tuna salad, tell them mermaids or sharks love this food. Only give one little tiny taste at first, rather than a big forkful, to avoid a tasting shock!*

↘ **art table** * *Help them make sculptures or pictures out of their vegetables, and then eat them up.*

↘ **count it** * *Make small mounds and have them count how many mountains they can eat.*

↘ **animal shapes** * *Asparagus can be dinosaur tails; beans can be little fish jumping into his mouth.*

↘ **look who's coming to dinner** * *Invite your child's stuffed animals or dolls to dinner. Set a place and make a fuss over how they love the food.*

↘ **stack it up** * *Stack foods high, and then take them down by eating one bite at a time.*

↘ **grow into it** * *Let your child wear a large shirt of yours and tell him he has to eat all of his healthy food to grow into it.*

↘ **favorite character** * *Tell them the food is their favorite character's favorite food.*

↘ **the wheel of mealtime** * *Very slowly spin the plate and tell them to grab something as it goes around.*

↘ **random associations** * *Say the food looks like something, such as, "These potatoes look like a poodle, don't you think?"*

toddler-friendly table tools

These are some ideas to get you to start looking at food presentation differently. Have fun trying out some new and unusual table tools. Try ethnic markets, craft stores, and gardening stores for supplies.

- ⬂ Try a deep, short-handled Asian soup spoon instead of a regular one.

- ⬂ Look for unusual items that can double as dishware, such as empty coconut shells, wooden sake cups, or tiny condiment dishes.

- ⬂ Trim a brown paper bag with decorative scissors for a place mat, and have your child draw on it while you are making dinner.

- ⬂ Look for biodegradable dishware made from corn or sugar cane—the kids will get a kick out of it, and you can compost it for the garden when you are done.

- ⬂ Make a place mat from clear contact paper placed over a page of an old illustrated book or child's drawing.

- ⬂ Make a bib from glitter pressed between two sheets of contact paper.

- ⬂ Use a cute bib. (Try Kangaroo Brand Products' hard plastic one—it catches everything.)

- ⬂ Serve small foods on decorative toothpicks, wooden skewers, Popsicle sticks, or lollipop sticks.

- ⬂ Check out a Japanese market for a wooden sushi board to serve dinner on.

- ⬂ Give your four- or five-year-old small real glassware to drink from, such as a shot glass or short drink glass, since they are harder to break.

- ⬂ Serve foods in small, kid-size prep dishes from a kitchen supply store. They are usually made from stainless steel.

- ⬂ Serve foods on parchment paper, wax paper, or in baskets.

tools in the kitchen

Make your life easier. There are some tools out there that will help make cooking much more pleasurable. Cooking tools can be really fun to use, and they can help make a rough time go more smoothly. Get rid of those old rusty strainers, dull knives, and half-melted spatulas. Check out this guide and see what you can find to make your life a little easier.

micro graters

- **scissors of all sizes and strengths** * This is the tool I reach for most often in my kitchen. I leave them out in a jar on the counter because my drawer would wear out from opening it and closing it all day long! Get a good-quality heavy-duty pair, a pair for cutting packages open, and a small pair. Make sure they are dishwasher-safe. To give them a quick sharpen, fold some aluminum foil and cut away; this will sharpen the blades.

- **food chopper or food processor** * Mincing food can be a monumental task and could make a person not want to cook. If you have a good-quality food chopper, though, you can mince with ease. Does your kid really care if his carrots are perfect 1/4-inch squares? No. I love my food chopper because it is small and easy to clean up. When I buy nuts, half the bag gets chopped and stored so I always have them on hand. Food processors are also handy for kneading dough and puréeing ingredients if you don't have a stick blender.

- **stick blender** * My most valued possession in the kitchen; I am not sure how people get along without this little gem. This is a must-have because it is easy to clean and quick to use. The recipes in this book are quick to make with this handy tool. If you don't have one, use a potato masher, food mill, stand blender, or food processor, depending on the recipe.

- **mallet or meat tenderizer** * This is the other tool I use almost every day. It quickly crushes ice, cereal, and stale bread for breadcrumbs. You will find yourself rummaging around for this tool all the time. If you can't find one, grab an old hammer or the bottom of a heavy soup pot.

- **knife** * A good-quality, sharp knife is a must. Cooking will become more enjoyable and less of a chore if you are not trying to cut your carrots with the likes of a spoon. A really good 8-inch chef's knife and a sharp paring knife are a great place to start. I also love having a few cheap serrated knifes around since they never seem to go dull.

- **tongs** * Put away that fork—there are tongs for that. I love this invention; get a good pair with a bit of rubber on the handle for easy gripping. A short pair is perfect for flipping meat in a pan, and longer ones are great for checking food in the oven.

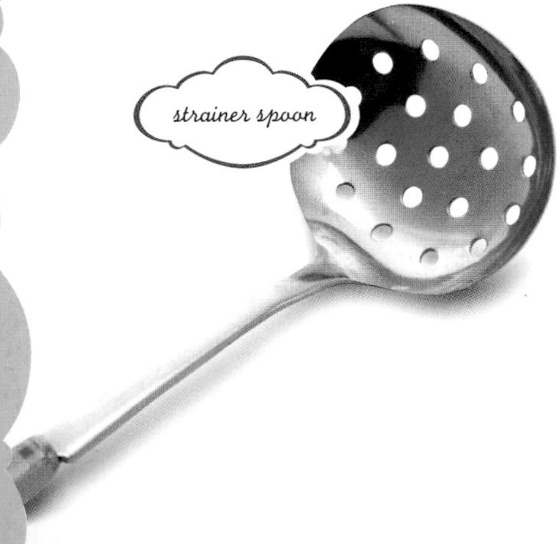
strainer spoon

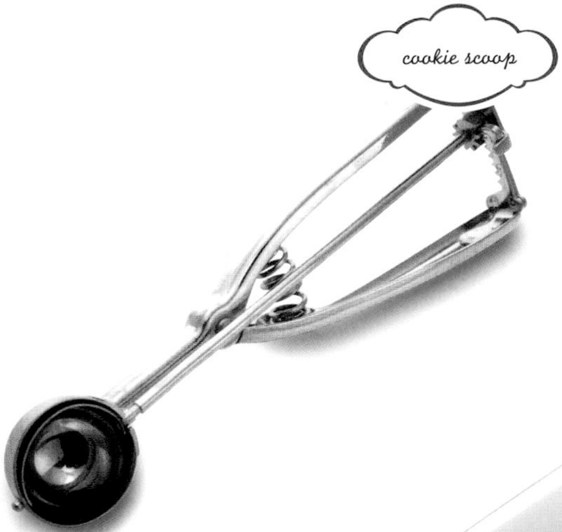
cookie scoop

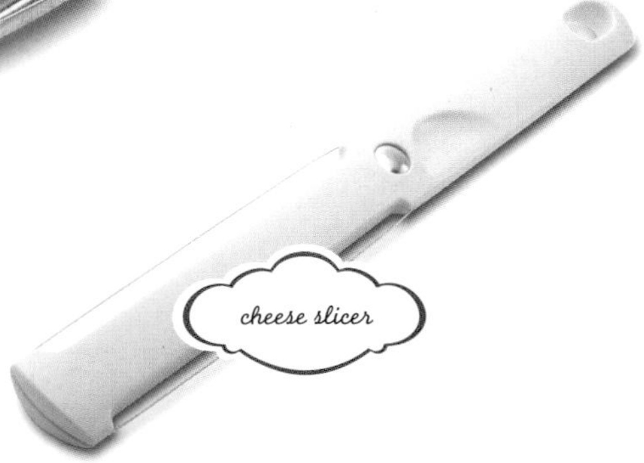
cheese slicer

micro grater * This is another leap in kitchen technology. If you don't have one, get one. This is a perfect tool to grate frozen ginger root, frozen cheese, carrots, chocolate, and citrus zest. There are different shapes; I like one with a plastic handle and flat grating surface. The face is basically a bunch of tiny razorlike blades, so grate with care and a smile.

rice cooker * Invaluable in the kitchen, it makes rice quickly and perfectly, putting an end to bland processed instant rice. With a cooker you can toss in anything you want, such as spices, herbs, or frozen vegetables, and it is perfect every time.

sugar shakers * These are invaluable in the kitchen; fill them with cinnamon-sugar, cocoa, powdered sugar, and wheat germ. This is a huge time saver for an instant sprinkling of fun. Try putting maple sugar in one; a little goes a long way.

high-temperature spatula * Forget scraping scrambled eggs off that old wooden spatula. It is the twenty-first century, so get yourself a silicone spatula. The silicone is nonstick and won't melt or burn, and they come in fun colors. They come in all shapes and sizes, too; the small ones are perfect for scrambling eggs or scraping cake batter from a bowl.

strainers of different sizes * These are so handy; you can use them for dusting foods with cocoa or straining out lemon seeds. Make sure you have tiny, medium, and large ones.

mini muffin tin * Makes kid-sized muffins, quiches, and tarts, and helps reduce cooking time, too.

mini tart shaper * This is a wooden dowel with a ball on the end that presses dough placed in a mini muffin tin into a tart shell. If you can't find one, wrap the bottom of a thick candle or wooden spoon handle in foil and use it in the same way.

small cookie scoop * This is a tool I use in many of the recipes in this book because it makes even-sized balls of dough or meat and keeps your hands clean.

good-quality nonstick pan * This will make your time in the kitchen much faster, and cleanup will be much easier. Get the best quality you can afford. As my friend Michelle says, "When you're trying to pass off those black flakes as pepper, it is time for a new pan"—not to mention that we shouldn't be eating that stuff!

sharp knife

spatula

- ↘ **apple corer** * Stop trying to cut out the hard part of the apple. Use a corer and make your life easier. Pop out the center of the apple, core and all. It also works nicely as a small extra cookie cutter.

- ↘ **apple wedger** * This tool cuts an apple into perfect wedges and cores at the same time.

- ↘ **box grater** * Usually a three- or four-sided tool for shaving or grating vegetables and cheese; perfect for grating fresh nutmeg or chocolate.

- ↘ **skewers or popsicle sticks** * You be the judge: Is your child ready for sharp, pointy objects? If you show them how to respect them and that they are not toys, then maybe? You can pick up lollipop and Popsicle sticks at kitchen supply stores and in many craft stores. Try putting bites of food on small fancy toothpicks or short skewers.

- ↘ **zip-top bags** * Fill them with pipeable foods such as nut butter or mashed potatoes, cut one corner off, and squeeze. Perfect for drawing designs, frosting, filling ice cube trays, or for condiments.

- ↘ **cheese slicer** • This tool is super when you buy block cheese; it makes perfect slices every time.

- ↘ **vegetable peeler** • Other than the obvious, this can be used on raw veggies to make ribbons. One of my favorite uses is on hard butter to get easy-to-spread slices, or on block cheese to make perfect curls every time.

- ↘ **small strainer spoon or spider** * Find these at kitchen supply stores or at an Asian market. They are small and perfect for poached eggs or pulling gnocchi out of boiling water.

- ↘ **bench scraper** * A flat stainless steel or plastic tool for scraping bread dough or chopped vegetables off the cutting board. Also handy for cutting dough such as gnocchi.

pantry essentials & smart shopping (don't be caught with your cupboards bare!)

I am not going to tell you to totally reorganize your kitchen. I'm sure you have enough to do already and, unless you are ready to hire a professional organizer, I bet it's not going to happen. Luckily, there are a few things you can do that will help streamline your time in the kitchen.

A well-stocked pantry is going to make you feel ready for anything. You should be able to see everything you have or your creativity won't flourish. Your brain is full of things like scheduling play dates and how much more garbage you can pack into the can before you really have to take it out. You want food fast, and this will make it easier for you.

First, use the shopping list in the back of this book. Make a bunch of photocopies to help you stay organized. Put it up near your pantry on a clipboard with a pen; if your pen is missing, you will never use the list. Write down items you need as you finish the food or as you are tossing out the empty container. Train other members of your family to write down foods as they finish them, too. This way you won't have to keep it all in your head or try to write a list on scraps of old paper while driving to the store.

The categories on the list are arranged by grocery aisle and can cut your shopping time down, especially if you are shopping with kids in tow. I know you don't want to go back to the store tomorrow! It can also help you remember what you have bought in the past. If you get in a rut, you can just look back at your old lists and see what ingredients you bought two months ago, but you have to save the lists! You will also have a stocked pantry of items to choose from so your meals will be right at the tip of your fingers. After you stock up, see if you can make a dish using this book as a guide and inspiration without having to go to the store.

This list will also help you save money and space by not buying what you don't need. How many times have you bought something—say a can of tomato paste or a packet of seasoning mix—only to find out you already have it at home? Space is a precious thing in your pantry or refrigerator, so don't overstuff them. Challenge yourself to use what you have on your shelves; this is where you can get really creative. You can learn how to shop for the things you will use frequently and not have the rest sit on your shelf going bad.

Next, keep the kitchen from becoming a complete disaster. A messy kitchen can really make someone want to order out! Cooking in a disorganized kitchen is not relaxing or inviting. According to the Web site Flylady.net, "If the kitchen is clean, the rest of the house stays clean, too . . . (If the sink is clean you are less likely to put a dirty dish in it.)" Our kitchen is constantly in use, full of meals, recipes, and toddler cooking experiments gone very, very wrong. The truth is that I was a professional dish leaver; in the morning when I walked into the kitchen, the first thing my eyes would focus on was dirty dishes! Seeing a dirty sink can trip a switch in your brain that makes you think of all the other things that are not done, making for a grumpy mommy. Flylady suggests you get the dishes out of the sink at night and wake up to a clean, empty sink so you can start your day much happier. I know some of you knew this already, but it was news to me. So now the sink is clean and dish-free before we go to bed, and in the morning I can spend time having tea with my family. Try it!

organic vs. nonorganic

Organic foods are grown without the use of harmful synthetic chemical pesticides and fertilizers. For a food to be certified organic, it must have been grown on farmland that has been free of such chemicals for a minimum of three years. When foods are grown using conventional farming methods, they can be subjected to enormous quantities of harmful chemicals, many of which have not been tested for safety and some of which are established as human carcinogens. In California alone, 400 million pounds of farming chemicals are used annually. Can you believe that?

eating organic

Try to opt for as many organic foods as possible when shopping. We are surrounded by thousands of chemicals, so why put them unnecessarily into our bodies? I can only suggest this way of thinking and let you decide. You may not want to or be able to buy everything organic. Organic foods tend to be a bit more expensive, but if you can manage to work in organic milk, fruit, veggies, and meat, you are off to a good start.

America's cupboards are bursting with food, but is it good, healthy food? Take a look in your own cupboard and see where you can begin to make a change. Read labels and you will quickly realize how much junk is in our food. Don't be afraid to change your shopping habits; your family will eventually thank you. Buy less and eat higher-quality foods. Take one step at a time and enjoy the change. Take responsibility to make the right choices for your family—that is the beauty of living in our modern society. We get the privilege to choose what to put into our bodies.

recipe notes

In some of the recipes I do not use measurements because it is about whatever you have on hand and getting creative in a simple way. I also err on the side of mild when adding spices, to get your kids used to the flavors. The idea is to up the flavors each time you make it. If you make it too strong the first time, they will probably refuse it next time.

ingredients

sugar

I have never seen a case of sugar deficiency, have you? We all know that our kids get way too much sugar. Sugar has its place; I am a firm believer in tasting all foods in moderation. But if you can cut down on sugary treats and stop rewarding with sugary snacks, you can make all of the recipes in this book without worry.

There are two ingredients in the world of food that can make or break a recipe. Ready for this? They are sugar and salt. They enhance the flavors of food but don't necessarily need to be used to make the foods high in sodium or overly sweet. If your kids are eating healthy snacks and natural ingredients, then you should have nothing to worry about. In countries such as Thailand, people use sugar in their savory cooking but don't eat sweets like we do here. Try to stay away from sodium-laced foods and processed sugary snacks. Try to use unbleached and organic sugar, maple products, or honey in these recipes, and you can feel good about the foods your kids are getting.

table salt vs. kosher salt

All of my recipes use flat-grained kosher salt. Table or iodized salt is fine grained, and a single teaspoon of table salt has more sodium than a teaspoon of kosher or sea salt. If you use table salt, these recipes will be much too salty. Get yourself a box of kosher salt and start to experiment with it. If you only have table salt, though, use about half as much as I've listed in the recipe.

the ketchup factor

Most kids defiantly think sugar-packed ketchup is a food group, so monitor their tomato-y intake. Buy sugar-free ketchup, or when serving condiments like sweet ketchup or pickle relish, use the drizzle or dot method. Make dots on all the food or on the plate, or draw a design and then put it away; they get the flavor but the food doesn't drown.

butter vs. oil & the fear of frying

You may find yourself thinking that butter and oil are bad for your kids, but our bodies need the healthy fats that occur naturally in nuts, avocados, seeds, fish, fresh butter, and unrefined olive oil. It's the trans fats and saturated oils that should be limited. These fats have been refined by high-heat processing, or hydrogenation, and these are the ones to steer clear of.

Butter is created from milk and has not been hydrogenated; it is perfectly fine in moderation. This is the "less is more" idea; great flavor using natural foods is a good way to start. When your child is over two years old, you can switch to low-fat dairy products. Extra-virgin olive oil is a great fat for kids and adults to have in their diet. Olive oil is also not hydrogenated and is full of essentials fats for brain growth and healthy skin. The more natural foods you use, the better you can feel about your child's health. Everything in moderation and your kids will be balanced and healthy and happy.

The fear of fried and fatty foods is rampant, but if you use fresh, healthy, unprocessed oils, you won't have to worry. If a recipe calls for frying, just add enough vegetable oil to the pan to coat the bottom and pan fry, flipping the food to cook thoroughly, and then drain it. The faster you fry, the less oil gets on the food, and the better it is for you. Make sure you have the oil temperature up around 350°F, and don't crowd your pan, as this will force the temperature of the oil down and you will end up with greasy food.

stock up: perfect pantry

Some of these recipes are based on traditional foods from many different cultures. The ingredients are readily available in the ethnic food aisles of the grocery store. Because I want you to try all kinds of flavors with your kids, I have added some more unusual ingredients into this basic list for you to try. There are so many fruits and vegetables to try, and this list is just a fraction of things to put in your cart. Challenge yourself to pick up a food or ingredient in the store that you have never used. Look around and grab anything you have never used, find a recipe when you get home, and go for it. The unfortunate truth is that most people only have about one hundred items they regularly buy in the store. That is a shame, since we live in a world where we can get any foods we can imagine but we tend to stick to what we know.

the freezer

Make sure you have a well-stocked freezer. The freezer is your friend so long as you know what's inside those mystery wrappers. Keep everything sealed and wrapped well, and keep a marker near you in the kitchen so you can note the date and contents on each wrapper. Arrange foods by sections inside the freezer: breakfast, meats, vegetables, snacks, and so on.

things to have on hand

⤵ *baking supplies*

Baking powder
Baking soda
Cornstarch
Flax seed, ground
Flour, unbleached all-purpose,
     whole wheat
Organic sprinkles
Peppermint extract
Powdered sugar
Semisweet mini chocolate chips
Sugar, organic or raw
Sweetened flaked coconut
Vanilla extract

⤵ *dry goods*

Bread crumbs, whole wheat
Cornflakes
Cornmeal
Dehydrated fruit or veggies
Desiccated coconut,
     shredded unsweetened
Dried currants
Dried split peas
Flax seed meal or whole flax seed
Instant potato flakes
Nonfat dry milk
Nut meal (finely ground nuts;
     you can make your own at home)
Panko breadcrumbs (from Japan;
     can be found in the ethnic aisle of
     your grocery store)
Quick-cooking oats
Steel-cut oats

⤵ *condiments*

Agave nectar: This is an ingredient
     that can replace honey or sugar in
     some cases. It is derived from
     the agave plant, and it has a low
     glycemic index.
Apple cider vinegar
Balsamic vinegar
Canola oil
Cinnamon sticks
Cooking spray
Dried dill weed
Dried oregano
Dried rosemary
Dried thyme
Dry mustard
Granulated onion or dehydrated
     onion flakes
Ground cinnamon
Ground ginger
Healthy (low-fat) dressings
Hoisin sauce
Honey
Hot sauce
Jelly, jam, marmalade
Ketchup, no sugar
Kosher salt
Maple sugar granules
Maple syrup
Nutmeg, whole or ground
Olive oil
Paprika

Peanut butter, or other nut butters
Pesto sauce
Plum sauce (a sweet sauce
     used in Asian cuisine)
Sesame oil
Sesame seeds, white and black
Soy sauce, low sodium,
     Chinese and Japanese styles
Unrefined coconut oil
     (great for spreading on waffles
     or mixing into rice)
Worcestershire sauce

⤵ *snacks*

Cereal, unsweetened or naturally
     sweetened
Dried fruit
Nuts, all kinds, salted and unsalted
Popcorn
Pretzel sticks
Rice cakes, with nori or plain
Rice crackers
Tortilla chips, white and blue

⤵ *rice, pasta, and grains*

Brown rice, long and short grain
Couscous, Israeli and regular
Egg noodles
Jasmine rice
Millet
Polenta
Quinoa rice pasta
Soba noodles
Spaghetti
Sushi rice

Tiny pasta stars or other
    quick-cooking pasta
Wild rice and rice mixes

canned foods

Beans, low sodium
Chicken and vegetable broth
Coconut milk, unsweetened
Healthy (low-sodium, low-fat) soups
Olives
Salmon
Tuna fish

miscellaneous

Gyoza wrappers, round
Tofu
Wonton skins, square

beverages

Carrot juice
Mango nectar

dairy

Block cheese, such as
    Cheddar and Jack
Brie cheese
Cottage cheese, small curd
Cream cheese
Goat cheese
Greek-style yogurt
Heavy cream

Milk
Parmesan, shredded and grated
Ranch dressing, all natural
Shredded cheese
Sour cream
Yogurt, plain or goat

frozen

Bay shrimp
Berries
Corn
Fresh ginger pieces, peeled
    and cut into chunks
Medium-size shrimp
Petite peas
Puff pastry
Spinach
Squash, diced
Sweet potato chunks
Turkey meatballs

meat

Bacon, all natural
Chicken breast
Deli meats, low sodium
Ground beef
Ground chicken or turkey
Sausage, chicken apple
    or breakfast variety
Smoked turkey
Turkey bacon

fresh fruit

Apples
Bananas

Berries
Dates
Lemons
Mangoes
Oranges
Peaches

fresh vegetables

Asparagus
Avocados
Basil
Beets
Carrots
Cucumbers
Garlic
Ginger
Green beans
Jicama
Mushroom caps, baby portobello
Onions, mild and sweet
Potatoes, all kinds
Romaine lettuce
Spinach
Squash, yellow
Swiss chard
Zucchini

baked items

Tortillas, corn and whole wheat
Whole-grain bread
Whole-wheat hot dog buns
Whole-wheat mini pitas

CHAPTER

01
vegetables

ingredients

8 ounces cream cheese

½ cup frozen petite green peas

Scant ¼ cup sugar

½ teaspoon peppermint extract

⅛ to ¼ cup semisweet mini chocolate chips

6 Popsicle sticks or wooden craft sticks

peas on a popsicle stick!? just tell them it tastes like mint–chocolate chip ice cream—but they are not quite ice cream and not quite vegetable. these are now a staple in our house—a great dessert, snack, or treat on a hot day. i just love it when a kid asks for a pea pop!

minty pea pops
makes 6 cube-shaped pops

preparation * Place the cream cheese, peas, and sugar in a microwave-safe bowl and microwave on high for 20-second intervals until the cheese is softened to room temperature.

Using a stick blender or standing blender, purée the ingredients into a smooth paste. Add the extract and mix again, scraping the bowl frequently. Stir in the chocolate chips by hand.

Place the mixture in a large zip-top bag and cut about ½ inch off of a bottom corner. Squeeze into a clean ice cube tray or mini muffin tin, place 1 Popsicle stick in each, and freeze until solid, about 1 hour. Depending on your freezer, you may have to let them freeze for up to 4 hours. For best results, make and freeze these overnight.

Once the pops are frozen, remove them from the molds by twisting just like ice cubes and seal in an airtight container for up to 1 month.

you won't believe they will ask for these over and over again. the peas worked so well i decided to expand the idea of frozen veggie pops and try sweet corn. they may even think these taste like mini frozen cheesecakes. no need for creative serving suggestions here, but feel free to try experimenting with different vegetables and ideas of your own.

corny veggie pops

makes 6 cube-shaped pops

ingredients

8 ounces cream cheese

¾ cup frozen yellow corn

2 tablespoons sugar

1 teaspoon ground cinnamon

⅛ to ¼ cup semisweet mini chocolate chips

6 Popsicle sticks or wooden craft sticks

preparation

* Place the cream cheese, corn, and sugar in a microwave-safe bowl and microwave on high for 20-second intervals until the cheese is softened to room temperature.

Using a stick blender or standing blender, purée the ingredients into a smooth paste. Add the cinnamon and mix again, scraping the bowl frequently. Stir in the chocolate chips by hand.

Place the mixture in a large zip-top bag and cut about ½ inch off of a bottom corner. Squeeze into a clean ice cube tray or mini muffin tin, place 1 Popsicle stick in each,

and freeze until solid, about 1 hour. Depending on your freezer, you may have to let them freeze for up to 4 hours. For best results, make and freeze these overnight.

Once the pops are frozen, remove them from the molds by twisting just like ice cubes and seal in an airtight container for up to 1 month.

variation

⬊ Put small pieces of graham crackers in the bottom of the ice cube trays and squeeze the mixture on top; the result will be more like a mini cheesecake.

potatoes are quick to make and very filling, but usually they take a long time to cool down, and your child may lose interest waiting. this is a great way to cool off a hot potato quickly so your kids can eat sooner. next time, add another frozen vegetable or some meat to the bottom of the potato. get creative with your toppings—the sky's the limit with a baked spud!

hot and cold potato

makes 1 potato

preparation * Wash the potato under running water, and poke holes all over it with a fork.

Place it on a microwave-safe plate and heat on high for about 5 minutes, or until a knife is easily inserted. If you would like to use a conventional oven, preheat it to 350°F. Bake the potato for about 45 minutes.

When finished cooking, split the potato down the center and, using a towel, squeeze the ends toward the center, creating an opening. Put the peas in the bottom, then put on a dollop of butter or sour cream and add more peas. The peas will thaw and create a cool, ready-to-eat potato.

ingredients

1 medium baking potato (about 5 ounces)

¼ cup frozen peas or other small frozen vegetable

Butter or sour cream, for topping

getting kids to eat raw vegetables can be a real struggle. this dish has crunch and texture from healthy vegetables, not chips! crisp lettuce is easier to chew than spring mix or bibb lettuce. give your child the small inside leaves so they will be easier to manage. make sure you break up the meat as small as you can, to make it easy to eat. have them fill the lettuce boats with the tasty "cargo" and sail them into the port (mouth).

sauce

3 tablespoons soy sauce

¼ cup water

1 tablespoon cornstarch

1 teaspoon granulated onion or 2 teaspoons dehydrated onion flakes

½ teaspoon kosher salt (optional)

⅛ teaspoon ground ginger

1 pound ground chicken, beef, or turkey

1 medium carrot, minced or grated

1 cup minced broccoli crowns and stems

1 head romaine lettuce, separated, washed, and dried

Chopped unsalted peanuts or cashews, for garnish (optional)

let us roll-ups
makes 4 servings

preparation * Put the sauce ingredients in a small bowl, stir to combine, and break up any lumps with a fork; set aside.

Heat a large sauté pan or wok on medium-high heat. Cook the meat, untouched, until it looks like it is cooking underneath and juices start to be released. Add the carrot and broccoli. Start breaking up the meat with a wooden spoon. Continue stirring and breaking up the lumps until the meat is thoroughly cooked. If the meat is giving off a lot of grease, drain it before adding the sauce.

Turn the heat down to medium-low, give the sauce a stir, and add it to the pan. Mix well and cook for 2 minutes more, until the meat

is coated and glossy, continuing to break up any large chunks of meat.

Serve the meat and lettuce leaves separately on a plate, and have your child try to put the meat in the leaves with a spoon, then sprinkle with nuts and eat like a taco.

variations

↘ Mix ¼ cup cooked rice into the meat mixture to change it up.

↘ Add minced onion or garlic when you add the vegetables. This will get your kids used to new flavors without them seeing the identifiable chunks. Then the next time you cook this recipe, make the onions larger.

ingredients

8 ounces (about 1½ cups)
frozen peas, thawed

2 tablespoons water

1 egg

3 tablespoons
all-purpose flour

¼ teaspoon kosher salt

⅛ teaspoon
baking powder

Vegetable oil, as needed

Butter or plain yogurt
for serving

these bright green pancakes are sweet and full of vegetables—a tender version of a regular pancake. inspired by a dish at a famous restaurant in new york city, these pancakes are delicate while cooking but sturdy when cool.

tell your kids that they look like lily pads and count them as they eat them. have them jump their fingers from one to the other like a frog. give them a small bowl of plain yogurt to dip into as they eat. the next time you make these, add some yellow curry powder to the yogurt. use petite green peas when possible; do not use canned peas for this recipe.

lily pad pancakes

makes 15 silver dollar size pancakes

preparation * Set aside ⅓ cup of the peas.

Add the remaining peas to a blender with the water and egg; purée until smooth.

Pour the mixture into a medium bowl and stir in the flour, salt, and baking powder and gradually mix with a fork or whisk. Stir in the reserved ⅓ cup peas; let the batter rest for 10 minutes while you clean up.

Place about 2 tablespoons of oil in a sauté pan, warm over medium heat until shimmering, and drop 1 tablespoon of batter into the pan. Gently cook for about 3 minutes, until you see bubbles forming around the edges. Flip and cook on the second side until very lightly browned. Continue until all the batter is gone. Serve warm with butter or plain yogurt.

recipe continues »

lily pad pancakes
continued

variation
↘ Add in cooked bay shrimp, diced chicken, or fresh corn.

toddler tip
If your child won't usually eat peas, make sure you add all the peas to the blender in the first step so they get puréed.

recipe note
↘ For regular yogurt containers on their way to expiring, take the top off, stir, and sprinkle granola over the top. Cut a slit in the plastic top and push a plastic spoon into the yogurt. Replace the top so the handle is sticking out, and freeze. When ready to eat, pop off the container, leaving the top on to catch drips.

these mushrooms are chewy and crispy, and have a surprise of hidden cheese in the bottom. the stuffing is made from plain old crackers—something most people have in the pantry. mushrooms are a neutral vegetable that really soaks up the flavoring they're paired with. these are so good that you may want to use them for your next dinner party! try baby portobellos or next time try goat cheese or a stronger flavored cheese, since it can stand up to all the stuffing.

top-o-the mushroom to ya

makes 4 servings

ingredients

1 tablespoon olive oil

8 ounces button mushrooms (about 12), cleaned and stems removed

1 tablespoon water

½ cup chicken or vegetable broth

12 rich butter crackers, broken in pieces

1 teaspoon dehydrated onion

¼ teaspoon dried oregano

2 ounces soft cheese, such as Brie (string cheese can be substituted in a pinch)

preparation * Preheat the oven to 350°F.

Heat a small nonstick skillet with the oil on medium-high heat. Place the mushroom caps top-side down in the pan and add the water. Cook, covered, for about 3 minutes. Uncover and cook another 5 minutes, until the caps look wilted. The caps should be full of water; drain each one into the pan using tongs, and set the caps top-side down onto a small rimmed baking sheet; set aside.

Over medium-low heat, add the broth, crackers, onion, and oregano to the pan. Cook, mashing with a fork, until all the liquid has been absorbed. Remove from the heat.

Put a small amount of cheese in the bottom of each mushroom cap. Using 2 spoons, drop a heaping amount of stuffing onto each cap, covering the cheese.

Place the baking sheet in the oven on the middle rack for 15 minutes. Raise the oven rack and broil on high another 3 to 4 minutes, until the stuffing starts to brown.

recipe note

↘ To clean mushrooms, dampen a paper towel and wipe the caps free of dirt. If you submerge them in water, they become soggy and flavorless.

ingredients

½ cup frozen spinach,
thawed and drained

3 tablespoons currants
or golden raisins

Chunk of Parmesan cheese

spinach, along with lima beans, is a vegetable that even some grownups wince at. many people have had bad experiences with these veggies. but they can be fantastic; it is the preparation that was probably all wrong. in spain, spinach is tossed with dried fruit and nuts to give it delicious flavor, and here is a version of that. teach your kids to like spinach by adding some dried fruit, soy sauce, or slivered almonds. it is a great vegetable; we all know what it did for popeye!

keep a bag of good-quality frozen spinach in your freezer for a back-up vegetable. toss it in anything from eggs to pasta. thaw it, put it in a bowl, and use scissors to chop it into small pieces. don't throw out those frozen stems—give them to the kids to munch on, and they may surprise you!

tiny spinach mountains

makes 2 servings

preparation * Mix the spinach with the currants. Heat in the microwave for 30 seconds to 1 minute, until warm.

Make very small bite-size mounds on a plate. Using a carrot peeler, make thin curls of Parmesan and place 1 over each mound.

variation

↘ Add 3 tablespoons toasted pine nuts after heating.

toddler tip

Unwrap 1 string cheese and pull down small sections of cheese, leaving a core. It should look just like a banana. Use your imagination; you can make bunnies, airplanes, and more.

this warm and satisfying spread has a chunky texture with a sweet and sour taste. this may remind you of thanksgiving, and you can use it as a stuffing inside chicken breasts or as a chunky dip. give your child a small spoon and tell them to "paint" the bread, letting them spread it on toasted bread all by themselves.

fruit and veggie spread

makes about 2 cups

ingredients

1 tablespoon butter

1 crisp apple, peeled and diced

1 cup frozen sweet potato pieces, thawed

3 pitted dates, chopped (about 1/3 cup)

1/8 to 1/4 teaspoon ground ginger

1/3 cup apple juice

1/4 cup chicken broth

1/8 teaspoon kosher salt

1 teaspoon apple cider vinegar

Sliced whole-wheat bread, for serving

preparation * Melt the butter in a saucepan over medium heat, add the apple pieces, and cook until they start to brown, stirring only a few times. When the apples are golden brown, add the sweet potato, dates, and ginger; cook, stirring occasionally, for 5 to 7 minutes, or until the sweet potato is softened. Add the juice, broth, and salt, and simmer, stirring occasionally, for 5 minutes more, or until all the liquid has been absorbed. Take off the heat and add the vinegar; stir to combine. The mixture will be slightly mashed but still a bit chunky.

Cut circles out of the bread with a sippy cup or 2- to 3-inch cookie cutter and toast them. Serve the apple spread, warm or cold, on toast rounds or as mini sandwiches. Store any leftovers well covered in the refrigerator for 3 days.

variations

❯ Try figs or prunes instead of dates, or use pears instead of apples.

❯ Add sliced turkey, chicken, or cheese on the sandwiches.

❯ Need to add some more sweetness? Try a few drops of pure maple syrup or agave nectar.

recipe notes

❯ Get date pieces from the bulk section of your store or fresh ones in the produce section.

❯ Cutting sticky things like dates? Spray your knife with cooking spray for a non-stick surface.

❯ Don't have a round cookie cutter? Use a sippy cup: take the top off, press the open end in the bread, and twist.

crisp and satisfying, and perfect for dipping, these are an easy version of the old standard potato pancake. adding squash gets kids used to a more complex flavor than just starchy potato, and it also gives a little crunch and a little squish with each bite. make them kid-size and they will be perfect for little hands. these are super served with applesauce, barbecue sauce, or sour cream.

squashed potato pancakes

makes 12 medium pancakes

ingredients

One 10-ounce box frozen squash, thawed

1 egg, beaten

¼ cup all-purpose flour

1 teaspoon kosher salt

1 teaspoon sugar

1 teaspoon baking powder

8 ounces frozen hash-brown potatoes, semithawed (about 10 minutes out of the freezer)

Vegetable oil, for frying

Applesauce, for serving

preparation * In a large bowl, mix the squash and egg together well. Add the flour, salt, sugar, and baking powder, and stir with a fork or your hands. Add the potatoes, stirring until combined.

Heat a nonstick sauté pan over medium heat, and add enough oil just to cover the bottom of the pan. When the oil is shimmering, portion about 2 tablespoons of the potato mixture into the pan and fry on each side until browned, about 6 minutes total. Remove with a slotted spoon and drain on paper towels. Repeat with the remaining batter and serve when the pancakes have cooled slightly. Serve with a cup of applesauce for dipping.

These can be refrigerated, well covered, for up to 2 days and reheated in a warm (250°F) oven.

variation

↘ Omit the salt and add ½ cup French-fried onion rings to the batter with the dry ingredients.

toddler tip

Ask your child to take a bite and tell you what they think the shape looks like—such as a bird, a boat, or a fish.

the creepier the better for some little kids! the bright green color of this soup will have them thinking about swamps. hide a slice of carrot or a bean in the bottom of the bowl, and have them dig in the swamp for a muck monster. this soup is packed with vegetables and will warm you up on a cool day. the more you blend it, the smoother and silkier it gets. serve with parmesan crisps.

you might want to make sure your child knows how to *really* use a spoon before you go on this adventure. this is a great time for a splat mat on the floor.

swamp soup

makes 4 servings

ingredients

4 cups chicken or vegetable broth, divided in half

1 medium onion, finely chopped

2 cloves garlic, finely chopped

1/8 teaspoon ground nutmeg

2 cups thinly sliced zucchini (3 medium)

2 medium ripe avocados

1/2 teaspoon kosher salt, or to taste

Prepared pesto (optional)

preparation * In a large saucepan, heat 2 cups of the broth, the onion, garlic, and nutmeg. When it is boiling, reduce the heat to low, cover, and cook for 15 minutes. Stir occasionally.

Add the remaining 2 cups broth and the zucchini and bring to a boil. Cover and reduce the heat to low. Cook for another 10 minutes, until the zucchini is limp but still bright green. Remove the lid and allow the soup to cool slightly.

In a blender, purée the soup mixture with the avocado flesh in batches. Return the blended soup to the pan and warm on low, adding salt to taste. Stir in pesto to taste, if desired.

recipe continues »

swamp soup

continued

variations

⬊ Use vegetable broth instead of chicken broth.

⬊ Add a dollop of leftover pesto to this soup after you blend it, and let your child stir it in.

⬊ Float toast strips on top and have a bean jump from log to log.

recipe notes

⬊ If your soup is still warm, leave the blender top open just a crack and place a dish towel over the whole top of the blender to prevent the top from popping off.

⬊ Entice your child with an easy home-made cracker to dip in the soup.

making parmesan crisps

Preheat a medium nonstick sauté pan on medium heat, and spray with olive oil spray or add 1 teaspoon of olive oil. Place 1 table-spoon shredded Parmesan cheese into the pan and spread it out to a thin layer with a spoon. Cook until bubbling, flip, and continue cooking for 30 seconds. Place it on a plate to cool. Repeat, making as many as you want.

kids love popcorn, and this soup has some floating right on top. let
the kids sprinkle on the popcorn as they eat the soup, and make
sure to have them listen to the sounds the corn makes as it soaks up
the soup. this can be a fun dish for the whole family.

popcorn soup

makes 4 servings

preparation * Melt the butter in a saucepan. When the butter has melted, whisk in the flour and continue whisking until the butter and flour are combined, about 1 minute. You are making a roux. It will start to smell like biscuits that are cooking; this is how you know it is ready. Do not let the roux get dark brown, but keep it light like the color of bread dough.

Add the broth and milk, whisking constantly to prevent lumps. Bring to a boil and reduce the heat to medium low. Cook for 10 minutes, until thickened. Add the corn and continue to cook for 5 more minutes, until the corn is thawed and the soup is bubbling.

Remove from the heat and add the cheese; stir until melted. Serve the soup in small bowls and sprinkle with popcorn at the table.

toddler tip
Have them count the corn on top of the soup before it sinks.

recipe notes

⬎ Roux is a blend of equal parts flour and butter, which are cooked and used to thicken soups. Roux can range from light blond to almost black, as that used in Cajun cuisine. Make a large batch and freeze it in ice cube trays, and store in the freezer for future use.

⬎ To pop a small amount of corn: Put about 2 tablespoons of popcorn in the bottom of a brown paper lunch sack. Fold the top down a few times and microwave on high until the popping slows, 2 to 3 minutes.

ingredients

3 tablespoons butter

3 tablespoons all-purpose flour

2 cups chicken or vegetable broth

1½ cups milk

1½ cups frozen corn kernels

*2 cups grated mild cheese,
or a combo including smoked
Gouda*

1 to 2 cups popped popcorn

O2
pasta and rice

these are colorful and mild-tasting, but they will make a mess, so you may want to eat them outside so you can leave the mess for the birds. your kids may even decide they love beets after trying these! rice balls are a very popular snack in japan, especially for kids. you can also make different shapes by forming them into triangles or flat disks. you can wrap them with thin sheets of dried seaweed called nori. kids like nori because it is crispy and salty and just fun to eat.

rainbow rice balls

makes about 12 ping pong–size balls
or about 2 dozen small balls

ingredients

1¼ cups water

1 cup raw Japanese sticky rice or white or brown jasmine rice

½ cup minced carrots

½ cup peeled and minced cooked beets, plus 1 whole, peeled

1 teaspoon kosher salt

Shredded nori (optional, see note on page 54)

Plastic wrap, cut into 3-inch squares

preparation * Mix the water, rice, carrots, and minced beets in your rice cooker and cook according to the manufacturer's directions. If you don't have a rice cooker, follow the stovetop directions on the bag of rice.

In the meantime, cut ¼-inch-thick slices of the reserved beet, then use a small cookie cutter to cut out about 12 beet circles. Place them on a plate as polka dots.

When the rice is finished cooking, add the salt and a handful of nori strips (if desired), and fluff with a fork. Using a teaspoon or small cookie scoop, drop the rice onto the plastic wrap squares.

Twist the loose ends of the plastic wrap so the balls of rice are very tightly compressed and there is a small "tail" of wrap hanging off. Let them cool unrefrigerated, then unwrap and serve on the beet polka dots.

recipe continues »

rainbow rice balls

continued

variations

❯ Substitute carrot juice for half of the water when cooking the rice.

❯ Add sesame seeds or cooked flaked salmon or shredded chicken.

toddler tip

Don't mention that the rice balls include beets until after they eat; just tell them they are rocks from outer space, and create a story about space aliens hopping from purple rock to purple rock.

recipe notes

❯ To work with cooked sticky rice, wet your hands before making the balls.

❯ Now you can get cooked peeled beets in the produce section of some grocery stores. If you can't find them, get about 4 ounces from the salad bar—just make sure they are not pickled!

❯ Nori sheets can be found in the ethnic aisle of the grocery store or at an Asian market. They do come preshredded, if you can find them. If you can't find them shredded, use clean kitchen shears or a very sharp knife to cut them into strips.

this dish will make your kids want to get up and dance, but only after they clean their plates! it is a take on the thai dessert sticky mango rice, although this one is a bit more savory. serve alongside sliced roasted chicken or broiled salmon. this is best in summer when fresh mangoes are sweet and juicy, but if you can't get fresh ones, try this recipe using frozen mangoes.

mango fandango
makes 3 servings

ingredients

1 cup raw short-grain sushi or jasmine rice

1 cup water

1 teaspoon sugar

One 8.4-ounce can mango nectar (see note)

1 teaspoon cornstarch

6½ ounces unsweetened coconut milk (half a can), shaken (see note)

Fresh mango, peeled and diced (optional)

White or black sesame seeds or toasted coconut, for garnish

preparation * Rinse the rice twice with cool water and drain. Place the rice, 1 cup water, and sugar in a rice cooker and cook according to the manufacturer's directions. If you do not have a rice cooker, cook the rice as directed on the package.

While the rice is cooking, pour the nectar into a small saucepan and whisk in the cornstarch.

Bring the mango mixture to a boil over medium heat, stirring frequently. Boil for 2 minutes, until it begins to thicken, then take off the heat and let it cool down to room temperature.

When the rice is finished cooking, pour the coconut milk over it and mix with a fork to combine.

To serve, place a scoop of rice in a bowl and drizzle it lightly with the mango sauce. If you have fresh mango, serve it alongside the rice. Let your child sprinkle sesame seeds or toasted coconut over the top.

variation

↘ This dish is also fantastic with crushed macadamia nuts or peanuts on top.

recipe notes

↘ If you do not shake the can of coconut milk, when you open it there will be a thick coconut cream on top. This cream is delicious and has many other uses, but for this recipe shake the can before opening, and the fat will be distributed.

↘ Mango nectar can be found in the beverage aisle or produce aisle of your local grocery store. It comes in cans and aseptic (shelf-stable) packages.

ingredients

One 12-ounce package wide egg noodles (see note)

½ cup (1 stick) butter

1 pound small-curd cottage cheese

1 pound sour cream

¾ cup sugar

4 eggs

2 teaspoons kosher salt

1 teaspoon ground cinnamon

2 teaspoons vanilla extract (optional)

2 cups crushed cornflakes (optional)

this side dish is a family favorite in many jewish homes and is always included in special celebrations. kugel, which means "ball" in german, originally referred to balls of noodle dough encasing fruity filling and steamed in covered pots—yum! some kugel recipes use dried fruit such as chopped prunes or dried apricots; some have nuts like slivered almonds, or the very popular addition of crushed cornflakes, but we like ours plain. it is certainly not everyday food. after it comes out of the oven, it is hard to walk by without picking a crispy noodle off the top, so that by the time it gets to the table it usually has holes all over it.

bubbi's krispy kugel

makes one 9-by-13-inch pan

preparation * Preheat the oven to 350°F and butter a 9-by-13-inch pan.

In a large pasta pot, boil the noodles in an abundant amount of salty water, slightly undercooking them. Drain and set aside.

In the empty pasta pot, melt the butter over low heat, turn off the stove, and mix the melted butter with the cottage cheese, sour cream, sugar, eggs, salt, cinnamon, and vanilla (if using).

Add the noodles and mix well, then transfer them to the prepared pan. Sprinkle the cornflakes over the top (if desired).

Bake for 45 minutes, or until bubbling and golden.

variations

⬐ Serve sweet with cinnamon-sugar or jam on top.

⬐ To serve savory, accompany with sour cream. You can really get creative with this recipe. Toss in whatever you have in the house, such as chopped dried apricots or prunes, slivered almonds, grated apple, or raisins.

toddler tips

⬐ Try more foods from different cultures. Never had smoked salmon? Give lox (smoked salmon) a try. Kids can surprise you with accepting new flavors—they may like it!

⬐ Once it cools, cut the kugel into small cubes and arrange them in a decorative pattern on the plate. Kids love bite-size portions; now you and your child just need to make up a story about the shapes. Are they bricks, or rocks, or stepping stones?

recipe note

⬐ Egg noodles can be found in the kosher section or pasta aisle of your grocery store.

does your child take the lemon out of your water and suck on it when you are at a restaurant? if so, they will love this recipe. it is based on something kids love—spaghetti—but with a twist to make it light and tangy. remind them of a time when they may have tasted the specific flavor in the past, such as lemonade, and they may be more interested in tasting this. let your child sprinkle more cheese on top all by themselves.

pucker-up psghetti
makes 4 servings

ingredients

Zest from half a lemon (see note)

½ cup grated Parmesan cheese, plus extra for garnish

⅓ cup olive oil

2 tablespoons fresh lemon juice (about 1 lemon)

1 tablespoon kosher salt

8 ounces cooked spaghetti, warm

preparation * Zest the lemon into a large bowl, then whisk in the cheese, oil, juice, and salt. Add the spaghetti and toss to coat. Serve warm with extra cheese for garnish.

variations

❑ Add ½ cup frozen spinach, thawed, or cooked white beans or grated raw zucchini.

❑ Substitute Japanese soba or udon noodles for the spaghetti.

toddler tips

❑ Tell them it is a bowl of worms and encourage them to slurp them before they slither out of the bowl.

❑ Let them sprinkle the cheese on themselves to keep them interested.

recipe notes

❑ Zest your lemon first and then cut it in half for juicing. If using only zest from half the lemon, zest the whole thing and freeze the remaining. Toss into a sauce or sprinkle on a cooked green veggie such as broccoli.

❑ If you are in a hurry, plug in your electric kettle and boil water for the pasta, then dump it into a pot on the stove and boiling will occur in half the time. Thanks Jessica!

the bright green color of this dish will interest even the most vegetable-phobic child. this sauce recipe is quick and can be added to any pasta or rice. suggest to your child that this is how monsters get that supercool green skin and maybe if they eat enough they will turn green, too. if your children have an aversion to peas, make sure you make a smooth purée, and omit the whole ones.

ingredients

2 cups frozen peas

¼ cup water

½ teaspoon kosher salt

¼ cup half-and-half

2 tablespoons butter

Cooked pasta or rice, hot

Grated Parmesan or other hard cheese

monster mash

makes about 2 cups

preparation * Place the peas, water, and salt in a medium saucepan. Bring to a boil and simmer for 2 minutes. Drain and set aside ½ cup of the peas.

Put the remaining peas, half-and-half, and butter in a medium bowl and blend with a stick blender or use a stand blender. Purée until smooth.

Fold the whole peas into the pea purée. Pour onto the warm pasta or rice. Serve with a dish of grated cheese and extra sauce for pouring or dipping.

variations

↘ Add cooked white beans, shredded raw zucchini, or cooked bacon or chicken to the pasta.

↘ Add dried dill or dried thyme to the sauce when blending. When adding dried herbs, make sure they have time to rehydrate by adding them into hot liquid or cooking them in the sauce. Dried, crispy herbs can be unappealing to eat.

homemade gnocchi are a great toddler food because you can flavor them with anything and they are easy to eat. this is a dish from italy that can be made in many different ways with tons of different ingredients; put your thinking cap on and start to get creative. there are much more complicated ways of making these, but this is very quick. i like to add pesto or sun-dried tomatoes to the dough.

knock knock gnocchi

makes about 6 small servings

ingredients

1 cup instant potato flakes

1 cup boiling water

2 teaspoons kosher salt, divided

1 egg, beaten

2 teaspoons to 1 tablespoon prepared basil or sun-dried tomato pesto (optional)

1½ cups all-purpose flour or 1 cup whole-wheat flour

Butter, olive oil, and grated Parmesan cheese, for garnish

preparation * Place the potato flakes in a medium bowl. Pour in the boiling water; stir with a fork until blended. Let cool slightly.

Boil a 4-quart saucepan of water. Once boiling, add 1 teaspoon of the salt.

Stir the egg, remaining 1 teaspoon salt, and pesto (if using) into the potato mixture. Blend in enough flour to make a fairly stiff dough. Turn the dough out onto a lightly floured board. Knead a few turns to bring it together.

Divide the dough in half. Shape each half into a long, thin roll, about the diameter of a nickel. With a knife or a bench scraper dipped in flour, cut the rolls on an angle into bite-sized pieces.

Place about one quarter of the gnocchi in the salted boiling water. As the gnocchi rise to the top of the pot, remove them with a slotted spoon and place them in a shallow serving dish. Repeat until all the gnocchi are cooked.

Serve warm with butter or olive oil, and Parmesan cheese.

variations

↘ Try adding 2 tablespoons goat cheese or shredded Cheddar cheese to the dough.

↘ Substitute vegetable juice, such as carrot, instead of water in the dough.

crispy gnocchi

If you want to use premade gnocchi, first cook them, then drain and toss into a hot sauté pan with 2 tablespoons of butter or olive oil. Let them cook on medium-high heat until golden and crunchy. Top with tomato sauce or another favorite sauce.

toddler tip

Get your kids to say "Knock knock gnocchi" five times fast every time they eat one!

recipe note

↘ Freeze leftovers such as pesto sauce, lemon juice, or coconut milk in small zip-top bags. Lay them flat to freeze, and then thaw as needed; just snap off a frozen corner to add to sauces or soups.

here is a very easy way to make homemade ravioli. gyoza wrappers can be baked, fried, or boiled like pasta. in this case, the wrappers cook up just like pasta, with a creamy inside. serve with browned cinnamon butter, or just plain as a great finger food. freeze extra pockets for those nights when the kids are hungry and you're too tired to cook. just boil, drain, and serve.

ingredients

8 ounces cream cheese

One 15-ounce can pumpkin purée

1 teaspoon kosher salt plus 1 tablespoon for pasta water

¼ teaspoon ground nutmeg (see note on page 66)

¼ teaspoon ground cinnamon

1 package (60) round gyoza wrappers (see note on page 66)

2 tablespoons butter

Grated Parmesan cheese

pumpkin pockets
makes 60 ravioli

preparation ✳ Place the cream cheese in a microwave-safe bowl, and heat on high for 30 seconds to soften. Add the pumpkin and stir to combine. Add 1 teaspoon of the salt, the nutmeg, and cinnamon, and mix with a stick blender or by hand until the filling is smooth.

Place a ½ teaspoon–sized ball of filling in the center of each wrapper. Wet the edges with water, and fold the ravioli over to form half moons. Pinch to close, pressing down lightly around the mounds of filling to prevent air bubbles.

Bring a large pot of water to a boil and add 1 tablespoon of the salt. Gently add the ravioli, and cook for about 4 minutes, stirring occasionally, until they float. (Depending on the size of the pot, you may have to cook them in batches.) Drain the pasta and toss them with butter and Parmesan.

recipe continues »

pumpkin pockets

continued

recipe notes

> ⬎ If you are cooking frozen Pumpkin Pockets, extend the cooking time to 6 minutes.

> ⬎ If you have whole nutmeg, use your micro grater or box grater to grate it into the filling.

> ⬎ Wonton wrappers are square and gyoza are round and slightly thicker, but they are essentially made of the same ingredients. You can use either for this recipe; cooking time will be longer for gyoza.

kids naturally like pasta, but sometimes even that's not enough to get them to the table. this dish is fun and gets them interested in the meal. they can dig through the bowl with their hands to find the pasta knots. little fingers can stir up the oil and vinegar to create polka dots perfect for dipping their pasta into; the more they stir, the smaller the polka dots get. this is a good introduction to the flavor of vinegar. plus, the kids can try tying their own knots, too.

pasta knots
and polka dots

makes 1 serving

preparation * Tie some of the spaghetti into double knots and place all of the spaghetti in a bowl.

Put the oil in a wide, shallow dish and add the vinegar to the middle, but do not stir. Have your child stir it up with their finger or a spoon to see the polka dots appear.

The more they stir, the smaller the polka dots will get.

Have them dip the spaghetti into the oil and vinegar, then into the cheese.

recipe continues »

ingredients

4 ounces or ½ cup cooked regular spaghetti, warm (see note on page 68)

2 tablespoons extra-virgin olive oil (see note on page 68)

1 teaspoon balsamic vinegar

Grated Parmesan cheese

pasta knots and polka dots
continued

recipe notes

↘ 2 ounces dried spaghetti makes 1 cup cooked.

↘ Adding oil to the pasta cooking water can produce mushy pasta; instead, add a large pinch of salt for flavor.

↘ Olive oil comes in many forms—extra-virgin is the first pressing of the olive and has the most flavor. It is best for dipping and using in dressings so you get the full flavor. It is not necessary to cook with extra-virgin, because you will lose the flavor and it can be costly. "Pure" or light olive oil is perfect for cooking; it allows you to use high heat and is healthy, too.

beans

stew can be a great way to get healthy foods into your child; potentially objectionable ingredients can be disguised and hidden easily. in south america, it is customary to add orange as a flavoring to black beans because it sweetens them and adds an unexpected and different flavor. you can thin this to a soup consistency by adding more broth or water. for a fun way to serve it up, cut an orange in half, scoop out the flesh, and fill it with stew.

sprinkle shredded cheese or diced avocado on top. try to think up silly names that rhyme with "stew" with your child, and they will be laughing so hard they will just eat it up!

ingredients

One 15-ounce can black beans, drained

1 cup frozen sweet potato chunks, thawed

¼ cup chicken broth or vegetable broth

¼ cup fresh orange juice

2 tablespoons tiny star pasta or ditalini (see note on page 74)

¾ teaspoon kosher salt

Zest from ½ an orange (optional)

starry night stew

makes 3 servings

preparation * Put the beans, sweet potatoes, broth, and orange juice into a saucepan, and bring it to a boil over medium-high heat.

Using a hand blender, purée the soup in the pan briefly, just about 3 seconds, to break up any big chunks of sweet potato. If you don't have a hand blender, mash the chunks with a fork or potato masher.

When the stew begins to boil again, add the pasta and salt and simmer about 8 minutes, until the pasta is soft. Take off the heat and add the zest (if using).

recipe continues »

starry night stew

continued

variation

↘ You can use any kind of bean for this recipe; experiment with different flavors.

recipe note

↘ Search out the pasta aisle; there are lots of tiny pastas and rice that you may have never noticed before.

this creamy dip is dairy-free and mild in taste. lentils and split peas cook very quickly and do not need to be presoaked. this dish can be thinned with coconut milk and more chicken broth for a delicious soup. use it as a spread on sandwiches, or serve on top of rice or meat. let your kids dip vegetables, chips, or pretzel sticks or pita chips into it.

bada bang bada bean dip

makes about 1½ cups

ingredients

1 cup dried yellow or green split peas (see note)

2½ cups water

2½ cups chicken or vegetable broth

1 shallot, chopped (see note)

1 clove garlic, smashed

¼ cup olive oil

½ teaspoon kosher salt

Cut vegetables, for serving

preparation * Place the peas in a saucepan, fill with water, and swish around; pour off the water and any debris. Add the 2½ cups water, broth, shallot, and garlic.

Simmer on medium heat, stirring frequently, for 35 minutes, until the peas are soft. Remove from the heat, and add the oil in a slow stream as you blend with a stick blender, stand blender, or food processor until puréed. Mix in the salt, and serve with the cut vegetables for dipping.

variation

↘ While mixing, add ¼ to ½ cup additional water to make a looser dip consistency.

toddler tip

Tell your kids this is a sandy forest and have them stick veggies or pretzel sticks into it as trees, then act like a dinosaur and eat the trees.

recipe notes

↘ Yellow split peas can be found in the bulk section of some grocery stores. You can substitute green split peas or red lentils. Black or green French lentils are not a good substitution for this recipe since they have an earthier flavor and a drier texture.

↘ Shallots are mild and sweet, and a good start for young children, who may think onions are too strong.

ingredients

2 cups cubed day-old
multigrain bread

Olive oil spray

1 cup cherry tomatoes, halved

1 cup canned, drained
pinto beans (half a 15-ounce can)

½ avocado, cubed

½ cup corn kernels,
fresh or canned

½ cup cooked ground beef
or turkey or sliced chicken breast
(optional)

¼ cup cotija añejo (see note)
or dry-aged cheese

2 tablespoons olive oil

¼ teaspoon kosher salt

a mexican take on an italian staple, this salad is a great way to use up old bread. this recipe can be cut down, but this is a perfect-size salad for the whole family to enjoy. the tomato juice gets soaked up in the toasted bread, making it chewy, not soggy. this is colorful, and you can use just about any vegetables or beans in it. it's super for a summer meal along with some grilled chicken, or dice the chicken and add it right into the salad.

pinto panzanella
makes about 10 servings

preparation * Preheat the oven or toaster oven to 350°F.

Spread the bread cubes on a baking sheet and spray them with the olive oil spray. Alternately, toss them in a bowl with 2 tablespoons oil. Toast the bread for 5 to 10 minutes, until slightly crisp, but not hard; remove from the pan and cool.

Put the tomatoes, beans, avocado, corn, meat (if using), and cheese in a large bowl, add the cooled bread, and drizzle with the oil and salt. Toss well to combine, and serve.

variation

↘ Try making a mild vinaigrette for kids by using 1 part vinegar of your choice and 2 to 3 parts olive oil. Add kosher salt and pepper to taste. Try using balsamic or apple cider vinegar for a different flavor. Use the vinaigrette in place of the oil and salt at the end of the recipe. Getting your kids used to flavorful dressings and vinegars will make eating more exciting for them and be easier for you.

toddler tip

Have your child pull out ingredients as they eat and talk about what shape and color they are.

recipe note

↘ *Cotija añejo* is a version of Mexican cheese that has been aged longer (*añejo* means "aged"). It is somewhat dry and crumbles easily; it also can be grated and used like Parmesan or dry Jack on salads or just about anything.

quick-cooking chicken

To cook chicken breasts or thighs quickly, use the sear and roast method. Preheat the oven to 375° to 400°F. In a small sauté pan over high heat, add 1 teaspoon oil, and season your chicken with salt and pepper. Place the chicken skin-side down and cook until the skin is a deep golden brown. Leave it alone; don't turn it over until it is golden. When golden, turn the chicken over and finish cooking it in a hot oven for 10 minutes, or until cooked through and no longer pink in the middle (internal temperature of 160°F). You can season it with anything; try curry powder, paprika, or a barbecue rub.

these look like chocolate, but they are made of beans! this is like a version of a chinese sweet bean dessert, but this one's made from ingredients you might have on hand. if you want to get crafty, you can always substitute authentic japanese adzuki beans, which come canned. this recipe is very forgiving—you can really go to town, making it taste different every time. this semisweet creation bakes like a cake and scoops into balls. it is so moist and delicious and is packed with fiber. be sure to dust the balls with powdered sugar to make them look pretty.

toddler truffles

makes about 24 balls

ingredients

One 15-ounce can black beans, drained and rinsed

½ cup sugar

½ cup packed brown sugar

½ cup finely chopped nuts

4 tablespoons (½ stick) butter, at room temperature

½ teaspoon baking powder

Pinch of kosher salt

2 eggs

Powdered sugar, for dusting

preparation * Preheat the oven to 300°F. Spray or butter an 8-by-8-inch pan; set aside.

In a large, deep bowl, combine the beans, sugars, nuts, butter, baking powder, and salt. Using a stick blender or food processor, start to work the ingredients around. When they are fully blended, add the eggs and blend to combine. Pour the mixture into the prepared pan.

Bake for 30 to 40 minutes, until firm and the edges get slightly crisp. Cool and cut into small cubes, or take a spoonful and gently roll into small balls in your palms. Dust with powdered sugar.

Store covered up to 5 days in the refrigerator.

variations

⬎ Substitute white beans, pintos, or adzuki beans. They can be found in the ethnic aisle of your grocery store. The texture and color may change, but the idea stays the same — a cake made of beans!

⬎ Add a tablespoon of orange zest, try different kinds of chopped nuts, or add dried currants after blending for a chunkier texture.

puff pastry is so versatile; it can be cooked up for sweet or savory dishes. keep a package in your freezer for quick meals or to cook up a snack. homemade puff pastry is delicious but time-consuming to make; the premade kind is perfectly good to use. just remember to let it thaw in the refrigerator before you try to use it. this recipe is reminiscent of the south american flavor combination of bean and banana—unusual but delicious.

treasure triangles

makes 18 triangles

ingredients

2 tablespoons butter or oil

2 bananas, sliced in rounds

¼ cup diced onion

One 15-ounce can black beans, drained

½ teaspoon kosher salt

One 16-ounce package frozen puff pastry, 2 sheets (see note on page 91)

1 cup shredded Monterey Jack or mild Cheddar cheese

Egg wash: 1 egg beaten with 1 tablespoon water

preparation * Heat the butter in a medium sauté pan over high heat. Add the bananas and sauté until golden. Remove the bananas to a bowl.

Add the onion to the sauté pan and cook for 3 to 5 minutes, until clear and softened. Add to the bananas.

Add the beans to the bowl. Using the back of a fork or potato masher, mash the bean mixture to a coarse paste; season with the salt and cool.

Preheat the oven to 425°F. Line a baking sheet with parchment paper or spray it with cooking spray.

Unfold each puff pastry sheet on a lightly floured cutting board. Cut each piece into 9 equal squares. Place 1 heaping tablespoon of cheese in the center of each square. Place 1 tablespoon of filling on top of the cheese.

Fold 1 corner of the dough over the filling to the opposite corner, forming a triangle. Using a fork, seal the edges of the dough. Arrange the triangles on a rimmed baking

recipe continues »

treasure triangles

continued

sheet; brush with the egg wash. Bake the triangles for about 20 minutes, until golden brown and puffed.

variation

↘ See what you have on hand. Try pinto beans and corn, or cooked crumbled bacon and a dot of peanut butter.

toddler tip

Tell them it is a treasure triangle and have them look inside to see if they can guess what the flavors are.

recipe notes

↘ Puff pastry is located in the freezer section of your grocery store, with the frozen pie crusts.

↘ Put the finished raw triangles in the freezer for 5 minutes before cooking. The colder the dough, the more beautiful the finished product. Unfilled baked shells may be stored in an airtight container at room temperature for up to 2 days.

↘ To recrisp shells, place them in a 400°F oven for 5 minutes.

these are protein-packed and slightly crisp. they are a great main dish. the batter will be very loose but will puff up perfectly. if you want to serve them as a sandwich, toast two small rounds of bread, add crisp lettuce, and serve like a veggie burger.

chickadee chickpea cakes
makes 12 to 15 silver dollar–size pancakes

ingredients

10 baby carrots or 2 large carrots, peeled (see note)

One 15-ounce can chickpeas, drained

½ cup frozen sweet potato chunks, cooked

½ cup all-purpose flour

1 teaspoon kosher salt

2 eggs

2 tablespoons vegetable oil

Ketchup, barbecue sauce, or shredded cheese, for garnish

preparation * Preheat the oven to 250°F and line a baking sheet with aluminum foil; set aside.

Put the carrots in a food processor, and pulse until they are in very small pieces. Add the chickpeas, sweet potatoes, flour, and salt, pulsing until combined but still slightly chunky. Add the eggs and pulse until combined.

Heat the oil in a sauté pan until shimmering, and turn the flame down to medium low. Using a tablespoon, gently drop spoonfuls of the batter into the oil and flatten them with the back of a spoon. Cook until golden brown, then drain the cakes on a paper towel. Place them on the prepared pan and finish cooking in the oven for 10 minutes, until firm to the touch.

Serve with ketchup, barbecue sauce, or cheese on top. Wrap well and freeze the cooked patties for future use, for up to 1 month.

variation

> Use black beans instead of chickpeas or use half black beans and half chickpeas.

> Use a total of 1 cup of sweet potatoes instead of carrots, and next time add a minced clove of garlic or one quarter of an onion to the food processor.

toddler tip

Tell your child this is what chickadees eat and have them chirp for more. Or pretend it is a Frisbee flying by and have them take a bite before it passes.

recipe note

> 10 baby carrots equals about 4 ounces.

mini drumsticks are easy to hold and not overwhelming for small hands. these can take minutes to marinate, but for the best flavor let them sit overnight in the fridge. use aluminum foil to wrap the ends to create a handle, adding more interest for your kids. if you can find old-fashioned chop frills or bonnets, put them on the ends of the drumsticks—kids love them!

marinade

One 11.5-ounce can mango nectar

¼ cup hoisin sauce (see note on page 88)

2 tablespoons ketchup

1 tablespoon honey

1 tablespoon cornstarch

1 teaspoon granulated onion or onion powder (see note)

1 teaspoon grated peeled fresh ginger

1 pound mini chicken drumsticks

Kosher salt

little drummerettes

makes about 20 pieces

preparation * Mix together all the marinade ingredients in a zip-top bag or covered container. Add the chicken and marinate for at least 1 hour or overnight in the refrigerator.

Preheat the oven to 400°F.

Drain off and discard the marinade. Pat the chicken dry, sprinkle with salt, place on a rimmed baking sheet, and bake for 15 to 20 minutes, or until golden.

Cool, and wrap the ends with aluminum foil for a fun and different kind of handle.

recipe continues »

little drummerettes

continued

toddler tip

Have them tap out a tune, alternating with a bite each time. See if they can follow a simple rhythm, making sure they eat in between!

recipe notes

↘ If you use granulated onion, your children will get used to the flavor of onion without having to maneuver around chunks of onion.

↘ Hoisin sauce is a Chinese cooking sauce that is thick, dark, and slightly sweet. It usually comes in a jar, and you can find it in the ethnic aisle of your grocery store.

eggs are a great way to get protein into your kids. start the day with a low-sugar, high-protein breakfast. this one will surprise them because it has corn chips in it. you can add guacamole or mild salsa on top. try adding blue corn chips for something different. this is a great way to use up the few chips in the bottom of the bag that no one is finishing. talk about what ingredients are called in different languages: in spanish, corn = *maiz* and eggs = *huevos*.

a-maize-ing scramble

makes 1 to 2 servings

preparation * Crack the eggs into a bowl and scramble them with a fork. Heat a small nonstick pan on medium heat, and add the butter. Put the eggs into the pan, add the chips, and stir until the eggs are cooked through. Add the cheese and serve.

variation
↘ Experiment with different cheeses and get your child to sprinkle them on and taste as they go.

ingredients

2 eggs

½ teaspoon butter or olive oil

4 to 5 tortilla chips, crushed

¼ cup shredded Cheddar, Jack, or añejo cheese (see note on page 77)

ingredients

One 10-inch sheet
frozen puff pastry dough,
thawed for 15 minutes at
room temperature
(see note)

2 tablespoons butter

2 tablespoons
all-purpose flour

1 cup milk

1½ cups (about 7 ounces)
frozen bay shrimp

3 tablespoons ketchup

1 teaspoon
Worcestershire sauce

½ teaspoon dry mustard

Kosher salt

Paprika, for garnish

this is a quick way to use frozen shrimp straight from the freezer. you'll make a thick sauce perfect by thawing the frozen shrimp right in the sauce on the stove. this dish is inspired by lobster newberg, a creamy lobster dish. it's cute and has a crispy, flaky dough to soak up the pink sauce. bay shrimp are sometimes sold as "salad" shrimp; keep some on hand to add to eggs, or eat plain.

sea biscuits

makes 4 servings

preparation * Preheat the oven to 400°F. Line a baking sheet with parchment paper or foil sprayed with nonstick spray.

Unfold the puff dough, and use a 3-inch cookie cutter or sippy cup to cut out 8 circles. Set 4 of them evenly spaced on the prepared baking sheet. Cut a smaller circle about

the size of a quarter out of the middle of the 4 remaining circles. Place the circles with the hole in them on top of the circles on the baking sheet. Bake for 15 minutes, until very puffed and golden. Set aside.

In a saucepan over medium heat, melt the butter, and whisk in the flour until blended and smelling slightly like biscuits, about 3 minutes. Slowly stir in the milk and continue stirring constantly, until thickened (it will be very thick). Turn the heat down to medium-low and add the shrimp, ketchup, Worcestershire, and mustard. Stir until the shrimp have thawed and the sauce is about as thick as yogurt. Season with salt to taste. Place each pastry shell on a plate and pour the sauce into the shells; sprinkle with paprika, and serve.

toddler tip
Pretend you are a sea horse, swimming down deep to get your snack out of the biscuit basket.

recipe notes
- To defrost puff pastry, move it from the freezer to the refrigerator 4 hours prior to use. You can also use the quick-thaw method: Separate the pastry sheets, covering each one with a piece of plastic wrap. Thaw the sheets at room temperature for about 15 minutes. Once thawed, do not leave them out, or they will become too soft to cut.

- You can make the puff pastry shells ahead and refrigerate them, covered, for a few hours until you are ready to fill them.

- Try sprinkling strips of puff pastry with Parmesan cheese and twist them before baking, or cut the dough into a square and fold in a piece of chocolate! Use your imagination—you can put just about anything in puff dough. Just remember to keep it very cold so it puffs well.

ingredients

*Cooking oil spray
or melted butter*

*½ cup dried
breadcrumbs or hazelnut
meal (see note on page 94)*

*4 ounces raw bulk
chicken-apple sausage
(see note on page 94)*

*¼ cup thawed and drained
frozen spinach*

1 egg, beaten

*1 Granny Smith
apple, cored and sliced
into ¼-inch rings*

*Ground cinnamon,
for dusting*

this is a great way to flavor a meat dish; if your little one won't eat meat, try this one—the apple flavor disguises it very well. serve them up one at a time so children are not overwhelmed; if they like it, serve up a few more. have them be the king of the rings and eat them up to keep them safe in their tummy.

lord of
the apple rings

makes about 6 servings

preparation * Preheat the oven to 375°F.

Line a rimmed baking sheet with aluminum foil or parchment paper and spray with cooking spray or brush with oil. Set aside.

Mix together the breadcrumbs, sausage, spinach, and egg in a medium bowl. Set aside.

There should be a hole in the center of each apple ring. Place the rings on the baking sheet and spray or brush each with oil or melted butter. Using a small cookie scoop or teaspoon, make 1-inch balls of the meat mixture and place one in the hole of each apple ring. Bake for 20 minutes, or until the meatballs are firm to the touch.

Place on a plate, dust with cinnamon, and serve.

recipe continues »

lord of the apple rings

continued

variations

↘ If you are crunched for time, use canned pineapple rings in water instead of apple slices. Dry them off with a paper towel before cooking, following the same procedure for cooking as on previous page. Pineapples and apples can also be grilled first before filling, for a different and delicious flavor.

toddler tip

Use plain yogurt as a dipping sauce. Ask your kids to stack the rings in a tower and see how high they can go; everything that falls has to be eaten.

recipe notes

↘ Nut meal is simply finely ground nuts; some stores sell it. To make your own, grind nuts in a food processor, stirring frequently to loosen the clumps. Store in an airtight container in the refrigerator or freezer.

↘ If you can't find bulk sausage, just remove the casings from uncooked link sausage.

tom ka gai **is a popular thai soup. this is a simple and fast scaled-down version. if you have leftover chicken, diced mushrooms, or angel hair pasta, toss it in. the best thing about this soup is that it is warm and soothing on a cool day; let them sip it out of a cute mug. make sure you grate the ginger, since biting a chunk will be too spicy for little mouths. add chopped, cooked swiss chard or fresh baby spinach leaves to the broth to change it up. pretend you are in a faraway place sipping this soup.**

thai'd up soup
makes 1 serving

preparation * Heat the broth in a child-safe mug by microwaving it on high for about 1 minute. Add the room-temperature coconut milk and salt. Grate 1 or 2 passes of ginger on a micro grater over the cup. Stir and serve.

variation

↘ Next time, try adding a squeeze of lime. Or add ¼ teaspoon of yellow curry powder to the soup.

recipe notes

↘ Freeze leftover coconut milk in ice cube trays by the tablespoon so when a recipe calls for it, you will know exactly how much to use. Transfer the cubes to a container and store in the freezer. Add to rice, soups, or smoothies.

↘ Keeping fresh ginger around can be tricky; it dries out or gets moldy fast. To have it always on hand, try this method: Peel it with a carrot peeler or scrape the peel off with the tip of a teaspoon, cut it into chunks, and freeze. Whenever you need it, just grate the frozen ginger using a micro grater. If using for a stir-fry, thaw it slightly and chop it into coins.

ingredients

½ cup chicken broth

¼ cup unsweetened coconut milk (see note)

Pinch of kosher salt

Frozen peeled fresh ginger root (see note)

filling

*8 ounces ground
pork or chicken*

*4 ounces medium
raw shrimp, shelled
(about ½ cup)*

1 green onion, minced

2 teaspoons soy sauce

1 teaspoon cornstarch

*½ teaspoon
grated peeled fresh
ginger (see note on
page 95) or ½ teaspoon
ground ginger*

30 square wonton skins

1 quart chicken broth

2 cups water

*Frozen vegetable
mix or other frozen
vegetable, as needed*

these wontons look like floating ghosts! they are mild in taste and sloppy to eat. once your kids learn to love this soup, they may want to be adventurous and order wonton soup when you go out. try floating very small pieces of frozen spinach in the soup, too. make a game out of it, and try to scoop up a slippery ghost.

soup ghosts
makes 6 servings or 30 wontons

preparation * Combine all the filling ingredients in the bowl of a food processor fitted with a blade attachment. Pulse to combine, making a paste. Or if you don't have a food processor, mince the shrimp with a food chopper and add everything to the meat, then mix with clean hands or a wooden spoon.

Fill a small bowl with water for sealing the wontons. Place 1 teaspoon of filling in the center of each wonton square. Using your finger, draw around the edges of the wonton skin with the water. Fold 1 wonton corner to meet the opposite and seal firmly. Next, wet the remaining 2 corners and pinch them together, pressing firmly. Or gather all

4 moistened corners together at the top to resemble a purse. Place the finished bundles on a plate.

Bring the broth and 2 cups water to a gentle boil; drop the wontons in, stirring gently, and cook for 5 to 7 minutes, until the skins are opaque and the meat inside is firm.

Place 3 wonton ghosts in a bowl with a small amount of broth and a handful of frozen peas or corn to cool it down.

variations

↘ Give them Asian-style plum sauce to drizzle into the soup.

↘ Try adding chopped canned water chestnuts to the meat mixture for a crunch.

recipe notes

↘ For a crunchy soup or salad topper, lay a small stack of wonton wrappers (about 5) on a cutting board. Thinly slice them into linguini-like strips, fry in a small amount of oil, and drain on a paper towel.

↘ To enhance store-bought chicken or vegetable broth, add onions, celery, carrots, parsley, a bay leaf, and chicken bones and cook for about 1 hour. Strain and enjoy.

↘ Ask your local grocery store for chicken bones to make stock, which you can use in place of broth. Sometimes they will give them to you for free or very inexpensively.

ingredients

2 boneless, skinless
chicken breasts, or 1 pound
chicken tenders

juice from ½ lemon

2 teaspoons cornstarch

2 egg whites

1 cup coarse, dry breadcrumbs
(or panko; see note on page 100)

½ cup grated Parmesan cheese

zest from 1 lemon

1 teaspoon kosher salt

2 tablespoons olive or
vegetable oil

kids need texture; it makes food more interesting and primes them for grown-up eating. this can be served warm or cold, and it is a nice twist on plain old chicken strips. lemon is a good way to get kids used to sour flavors.

twistin' chicken

makes about 12 tenders

preparation * Cut the chicken lengthwise into ½-inch-wide strips. Mix together the lemon juice and cornstarch, then mix in the egg whites; set aside.

For the breading: Combine the breadcrumbs, cheese, zest, and salt in a low, wide dish or zip-top bag. Dip the chicken in the egg mixture and then into the breading mixture. Place onto a plate and set aside.

Heat a sauté pan on medium heat and add the oil. Sauté the chicken strips until golden on both sides.

variations

↘ Try lime or orange juice and zest instead of lemon.

↘ Use turkey breast in place of chicken.

recipe continues »

twistin' chicken

continued

toddler tip

Let them twist some lemon juice on it and then see if eating the chicken can make them do the Twist. After dinner, put some music on and dance!

recipe notes

↘ Use your child's favorite dipping sauce, such as ranch or barbecue, to dunk these into. Mayonnaise with a bit of dried mustard and lemon zest is yummy, too.

↘ Freeze your chicken slightly to make it easier to slice.

↘ If you are concerned about thoroughly cooking your chicken, put it in a 300°F oven on a baking sheet to finish cooking for about 5 minutes.

↘ Panko breadcrumbs are from Japan and can be found in the ethnic aisle of your grocery store.

kids will love this surprise package. it is small and manageable, and you can use up any vegetable you have; just make sure to make them small enough to keep the cooking time short. serve with brown rice mixed with chickpeas, and unsweetened shredded coconut on top. open these packages at the table for a deep-sea surprise.

shrimp boats

makes 4 servings

ingredients

8 ounces medium raw shrimp (about 20)

½ cup finely chopped or grated carrots, zucchini, or snow peas

½ cup full-fat unsweetened coconut milk (shake can before opening)

10 basil leaves, torn (see note)

Kosher salt

preparation * Preheat the oven to 350°F.

Tear 4 pieces of aluminum foil into 8-inch squares. Curl up the sides of the foil loosely so the ingredients will be in the center. Place the foil on a rimmed baking sheet.

Put about 5 shrimp into each packet; sprinkle 2 tablespoons of the carrots, 2 tablespoons of the coconut milk, and some basil over each shrimp packet. Sprinkle with salt. Fold the packets closed so no air can get out. Bake for 10 to 12 minutes, until the shrimp are firm and pink.

Remove from the oven, being careful of the steam as you open the packets. Serve on a plate in the foil, and have your kids watch the show as you open the packages at the table.

recipe note

↘ To save fresh basil, purée it in your food processor while streaming in olive oil to make a loose paste. Freeze in ice cube trays, transfer to a storage bag, and keep in the freezer. Add to sautéed meats and soups, or spread on warm toasted bread.

ingredients

Olive oil spray

One 14-ounce package firm tofu, cut into ½-inch slices (see note)

½ cup whole-wheat or all-purpose flour

¼ cup fine cornmeal

½ teaspoon kosher salt

⅛ to ¼ teaspoon dry mustard

marinade

2 tablespoons hoisin sauce (see note)

2 tablespoons soy sauce

1 tablespoon water

dipping sauce

2 tablespoons apricot or orange marmalade

2 teaspoons balsamic vinegar

¼ cup water

½ teaspoon cornstarch

tofu is protein-rich and can be used in many different ways. you can marinate, bake, fry, grill, broil, and boil it. this recipe gives flavor to a food that can be lacking in that area. marinating it and then baking it to get a crispy result will have them asking for more.

i heart tofu

makes 6

preparation * Preheat the oven to 400°F. Prepare a baking sheet by spraying it with olive oil spray. Using a small 2- to 3-inch heart-shaped cookie cutter, cut out as many hearts from the tofu slices as you can. If you don't have a cutter, just use a drinking glass to cut circles.

Mix together the hoisin sauce, soy sauce, and water in a low wide dish; add the tofu hearts or circles, and marinate them at room temperature for about 15 minutes, or refrigerate for up to 2 hours.

Mix together the flour, cornmeal, salt, and mustard in a shallow dish. Drain the tofu hearts and place them in the breading mixture to coat well. Lay out the hearts on the prepared baking sheet, spray the tops with the olive oil spray, and bake for 15 minutes, until crisp.

Meanwhile, place the marmalade and balsamic vinegar in a very small saucepan over low heat. Mix the water and cornstarch together, and stir them into the pan. Bring to a boil, stirring constantly. Once boiling, the sauce will thicken; cook for 2 minutes. Remove from the heat and cool.

Serve the crisp tofu hearts with a big "I love you," a smile, and the dipping sauce.

recipe notes
↘ Save the scraps from cutting out the tofu and refrigerate them for later use in a

stir-fry or egg scramble. Tofu will last, refrigerated in water, for about 4 days.

↘ Freezing tofu will make it chewier and give it a meatier texture that can be disguised in many ways. Crumble and add to scrambled eggs, meat loaf, or veggie burgers. The day before you want to cook, simply defrost the tofu in the fridge.

↘ Hoisin sauce is a condiment used in Chinese and Vietnamese cooking. It is a sweet soybean-based sauce with garlic and hints of ginger.

O5
sandwiches

this sandwich is a classic, but done this way it is a real surprise and a fun way to make the same old grilled cheese. the genius of the waffle iron is that it cooks evenly on both sides simultaneously, saving you time in the end. it comes out crispy, crunchy, and cheesy— something the kids are sure to think is really silly. have a variety of cheeses on hand to get them used to goat cheese and others they may not have had. a belgian waffle maker works best, but a standard one works, too. be prepared—the cheese may ooze out of the waffle iron. this recipe serves two because you won't be able to resist eating one yourself.

ingredients

4 slices soft whole-wheat bread

2 tablespoons butter, softened

4 slices Cheddar or Monterey Jack cheese

waffle grilled cheese

makes 2 sandwiches

preparation * Place a sheet of aluminum foil underneath a nonstick waffle iron to aid in cleanup, just in case the cheese oozes. Preheat it as directed by the manufacturer.

Assemble the sandwiches by buttering the outside slices of the bread and placing the cheese slices on the insides.

When the waffle iron is hot, put the sandwiches in the waffle iron and close it. Cook for 2 to 3 minutes, or until the undersides are golden brown and the cheese is oozing. Peek once or twice to make sure they are not getting overcooked. No need to flip these because they will cook evenly on both sides. Remove the sandwiches with tongs or a fork and cool slightly before little hands touch them.

recipe continues »

waffle grilled cheese

continued

variations

↘ Try adding a bit of smoked mozzarella or fontina cheese.

↘ Try adding a slice of deli meat or thinly sliced tomato.

recipe note

↘ To clean your waffle iron, lay a damp paper towel in the hot waffle iron for a few seconds to steam the leftover grunge, and use a Q-tip to clean out the crevices.

warm slices of apple on bread with cheese—what could be better?

a is for
apple and cheese

makes 1 sandwich

ingredients

1 tablespoon butter

1 crisp apple, cored and cut into thin half moons or rounds

2 slices mild Cheddar cheese, cut into 3-inch circles

2 slices bread, cut into 3-inch circles

preparation * Heat a small sauté pan on medium heat, and add the butter; cook until bubbly. Cook a few slices of the apple until they get soft and start to brown, about 2 minutes. Flip over and cook the other sides. Place the cheese on a slice of bread, then top with warm apple slices and more cheese. Place the top piece of bread on the sandwich and serve.

toddler tip

This makes a great opportunity to teach the ABC's: A is for apple, B is for bread, C is for cheese. As they eat, keep the alphabet going!

variation

↘ Add cooked sausage, a slice of turkey, or thinly sliced carrot to the sandwich.

recipe note

↘ Need to slice cheese thinly? Use a carrot peeler to make ribbons.

ingredients

1 whole-wheat mini pita bread

1 egg, scrambled (see note)

1 slice mild Cheddar cheese

2 tablespoons cooked sausage or diced cooked bacon or crumbled firm tofu

middle eastern pita bread is the perfect vehicle for any filling like vegetables (raw or cooked), meats, and spreads. use the large-size pita pockets and cut them in half, or get the mini ones just right for smaller hands.

this will get your kids interested in breakfast again—use eggs as the base and add whatever tasty ingredients you can dream of. this recipe is just a jumping-off point to create your own favorite creation. once you have pita, vegetables, and some protein, the possibilities are endless. ask the kids, "would you put eggs in your pockets?" they will laugh and be interested in what you're serving.

my pocket's full of eggs!

makes 1 sandwich

preparation * Preheat the oven or toaster oven to 350°F.

Cut the top quarter off the pita to form a pocket. Stuff the cut top upside down into the bottom of the pita, wrap it in aluminum foil and heat in the oven for about 5 minutes. Remove it from the oven and stuff with the egg, cheese, and sausage, and serve.

recipe notes

↘ If you are making a bunch of sandwiches, wrap them in foil and hold in a 200°F oven to keep them warm and soften the bread.

- Use leftover pita as a base for pizza, or cut into triangles and rub with olive oil, sprinkle with salt, and bake at 350°F for 5 to 7 minutes for chips.
- You can scramble an egg in the microwave in a microwave-safe container. Cook on high for 1 to 2 minutes, giving it a stir every 30 seconds.

in a pinch, a plain old banana can become a hot dog! this is a funny and different way to serve this fruit. put it in front of your child and watch their reaction. let your kids help add the "mustard"—it may be messy, but it is sure to get them interested. and it's a great way to use up your old hamburger or hot dog buns. serve with banana chips for the ultimate tropical experience.

banana hot dog

makes 1 serving

preparation * Place the peeled banana in a bun. Fill 2 zip-top bags, 1 with jelly and the other with peanut butter. Cut a tiny hole in the corner of each bag, and squeeze out onto the banana as you would mustard and ketchup.

Eat and enjoy.

variations
↘ Add crushed pistachios for a crunchy relish look-alike.

↘ Cereal and dried fruit make great additional toppings.

toddler tip
↘ Let your toddler have some fun squeezing out the peanut butter and jelly in crazy patterns on their plates.

recipe note
↘ If you are weary of peanut butter, try soy nut or almond butter for a change.

ingredients

1 banana, peeled

1 whole-wheat hot dog bun

Jelly

Creamy peanut butter

ingredients

*2 slices whole-grain bread
or leftover hot dog buns*

2 tablespoons peanut butter

2 tablespoons jelly

¼ cup milk or heavy cream

1 egg

1 tablespoon butter

here's a decadent sandwich you will find yourself nibbling on as you serve it. warm sandwiches are so comforting, and this one is great for either breakfast or lunch. it has lots of protein from the added egg and milk.

pb&j french toast

makes 1 sandwich

preparation * Spread the peanut butter on 1 slice of bread. Spread the jelly on the other slice of bread. Put the 2 slices together to form a sandwich.

In a shallow bowl, lightly whisk the milk and egg together. Soak the sandwiches in the egg mixture for 1 to 2 minutes per side, letting the mixture soak in well.

Melt the butter in a sauté pan over medium heat. Brown both sides of the sandwich, about 4 minutes per side until golden.

Cut into quarters and stack them on a plate to serve.

recipe notes

⬊ If you find your French toast too wet in the center, place it in a 300°F oven for 5 minutes, and it will cook through perfectly.

⬊ This recipe is easily multiplied to make more sandwiches.

CHAPTER

06
fruit

your child is hungry and asking for breakfast, but the oatmeal is so hot it might as well be molten lava! no need to make your child wait—use this simple method to cool it off quickly. add flavor and decrease the temperature with frozen fruit (and you won't need the sugar). make sure to have a bib handy for this one!

berry cool oatmeal

makes 1 serving

preparation * Cook the oatmeal as directed on the package. Drop the frozen blueberries into the hot oatmeal for a quick cooling effect. By the time you place the bowl in front of your child, it will be ready to eat.

toddler tip

↘ Have your child stir and see the oatmeal turning purple.

↘ Add a splash of milk to create even more purple color (and additional calcium!).

recipe notes

↘ Freeze fruit such as berries, overripe bananas, or mangoes in small chunks to cool oatmeal, or use in smoothies; fruit with high water content, such as melon or stone fruits, tend not to freeze well.

↘ Instant oatmeal can lack texture; try steel-cut or Irish oats. You can soak them overnight on the stove and cook them quickly in the morning. They are hearty and delicious, and stick to your ribs.

ingredients

1 serving hot oatmeal or hot cereal of your choice

¼ cup frozen wild blueberries, bananas, or other frozen fruit (see note)

this fruit salad is cut into small pieces, so it's fun and easy to eat. the sweet tortilla chips add a great crunch with the soft fruit. serve as "chips and dip," or spoon it over mild white fish or serve alongside chicken.

confetti de fruta

makes 2 servings

ingredients

1 cup diced organic strawberries

½ cup diced fresh peaches

¼ cup diced crisp apple or jicama

1 teaspoon balsamic vinegar

2 large flour tortillas

2 tablespoons butter, melted

Cinnamon-sugar, for sprinkling

preparation ∗ Preheat the oven to 350°F.

Combine the fruits and vinegar in a medium bowl and mix gently with a spoon.

While the fruit is macerating, make the tortilla chips. Brush the tortillas with the butter and sprinkle with a generous amount of cinnamon-sugar. Place the tortillas on a baking sheet and bake for 12 minutes, or until golden brown and crisp. When cool, break the chips into manageable pieces and serve with the fruit.

variation

❯ In the summer, add very ripe cherry tomatoes, cut in half or quartered, to give this a slightly different tangy flavor.

toddler tip

❯ Ask your child if they can shovel up the "confetti" with the chips!

❯ Serve a slice of apple to use as a food pusher or "shovel" to help get the salsa onto the chip.

recipe continues »

confetti de fruta

continued

quick-cooking fish

To cook a piece of salmon or other hearty fish quickly, use the sear and roast method. Preheat the oven to 375°F. In a small sauté pan over high heat, add 1 teaspoon oil, and season your fish with salt and pepper. Cook the fish top-side down. Leave it alone; don't turn it over until it is golden. Turn the fish over and finish cooking it in the oven for 5 to 10 minutes, or until cooked through and it no longer looks raw (internal temperature of 140°F).

yes, it's a fruit! avocados are a great source of the good kind of fat you want your kids to eat. they are technically a fruit and kids like fruit, so be sure to tell them that! in indonesia, it is common to prepare an avocado shake (see below). try it, you'll like it. when choosing an avocado, pop off the little hard stem end, and if you see green underneath, it is a good one. if you see black underneath, keep looking. pick one that is slightly soft, not mushy. i call for dehydrated corn here because unlike dried vegetables or fruits, all the water has been extracted, making it easy to crush.

avocado dippers
makes 3 servings

preparation * Cut the avocado in half and remove the pit. Cut each half into ½-inch cubes and put 1 on each skewer or Popsicle stick. (Or just let your child dip the avocado with no stick.)

Place the corn or cereal in a zip-top bag and crush with a mallet or the bottom of a small heavy pan. Dip the skewers into the crushed ingredient of your choice.

variation

↘ Serve the skewers stuck into half an orange so they are sticking out. Let your child grab one and dip it into each topping.

recipe note

↘ Dehydrated fruits and vegetables are a healthy, quick snack and are easy to crush. They can be found in the produce section or bulk section of most grocery stores.

avocado milkshake

1 medium avocado, peeled and seeded / 2 cups ice cubes / ⅓ cup milk / up to 3 tablespoons sweetened condensed milk, depending on sweetness of avocado

Place all the ingredients in a blender and blend until the ice is completely crushed and the drink is thick and foamy.

ingredients

1 ripe avocado

Short skewers or Popsicle sticks

½ cup dehydrated corn or other vegetable, frosted flakes, or shredded wheat cereal

no need to cook this one! it's fast, easy, and—best of all—it's natural. it's also tasty on top of pancakes or cereal. a micro grater will make the apple deliciously mushy and juicy. if you don't have one, a regular box grater will do nicely.

split-second applesauce

makes 1 serving

ingredients

*Juice from
¼ to ½ lemon*

1 firm apple

*¼ teaspoon
ground cinnamon*

preparation * Place the lemon juice into the bottom of a small bowl. Using a micro grater, grate the apple into the lemon juice. Mix in the cinnamon and eat.

variation

⬃ Add currants, shredded carrots, or crushed pecans to the mix.

toddler tip

Tell your child it is food that horses love. Plan a trip to see a real horse, and feed it an apple. Or get a book on horses from the library. Neigh . . .

recipe note

⬃ Adding dehydrated fruit to sugar cuts the amount of sugar you will need to sprinkle on top of foods. To make fruit sugar, put 1 cup granulated sugar in a food processor. Add 1 cup dehydrated fruit, such as strawberries or blueberries, and process until all the fruit is pulverized. Store in an airtight container. Sprinkle on muffin batter, cakes, or too-tart applesauce.

it's healthy, cold, and refreshing—it's frozen yogurt! this is a great way to use up leftover fruit and yogurt. in the summertime, you can usually find popsicle molds at the drugstore or grocery store.

claire's coconut ice

makes four 3.25-ounce pops

preparation * Place the bananas, yogurt, and coconut into the blender. Blend until all ingredients are combined into a liquid; it will not be completely smooth because of the shredded coconut. Carefully pour the liquid into the molds and place the tops or wooden craft sticks into the center of each one.

Place the molds in the freezer on a level surface to set; this will take about three hours. When solid, remove from the freezer and serve.

variation

↘ Substitute 1 cup sliced strawberries for the bananas. Substitute blueberry or lime yogurt for the vanilla.

recipe note

↘ To loosen the popsicles, run room-temperature water over the sides of the molds.

ingredients

1 large ripe banana, peeled

¾ cup vanilla yogurt

½ cup shredded sweetened coconut

this cool soup is great for hot summer days and has protein, calcium, and lots of tasty blackberries. yogurt is a staple of many cultures, from greece to india, and is great to keep on hand for dishes like this. greek-style yogurt is particularly thick and creamy and makes terrific sauces and other sweet dishes. explain to your child that soup isn't always hot—this one will taste like dessert.

black and blue soup

makes 2 cups

preparation * Combine the yogurt, blackberries, half-and-half, sugar, and honey in a bowl, and purée with a stick blender or in a regular blender until the mixture is very smooth. Pour into small bowls, garnish with more berries, and serve.

toddler tip

This one can be a real mess, so give your child a straw and let them try to drink it.

recipe notes

↘ Try plain yogurt on chicken or with diced cucumbers, dill, and kosher salt mixed in as a dip.

↘ Is the expiration date on your individual yogurt tubes sneaking up on you? Toss them in the freezer for a cool treat, and use in place of ice in your child's lunchbox.

↘ If you have trouble getting Greek-style yogurt, ask your grocer to order it for you. To make your own thickened yogurt in a pinch, place regular plain yogurt in a coffee filter inside a strainer. Place the strainer in a bowl, cover with a cloth, and let it rest in the refrigerator overnight.

ingredients

Two 5.3-ounce containers thick plain Greek-style yogurt (about 1¼ cups; see note)

4 ounces (1 cup) frozen blackberries, thawed

¼ cup half-and-half or whole milk

2 tablespoons sugar

2 teaspoons honey

Extra berries, for garnish

CHAPTER

07

snack attack

**use ingredients
such as:**

¼ cup large-flake
coconut

½ cup dried kiwi, diced

½ cup dried pineapple

½ cup dried cherries

½ cup dried
raspberries

½ cup dried blueberries

¼ cup cashew
pieces or pine nuts
(see note)

½ cup leftover cereal

tell the children it's time to be important explorers who need some healthy snacks to bring with them on the trek. this is a great way to use up all those half-empty packages in your pantry. dehydrated foods are healthy and easy for small hands to pick up and eat. get adventurous—look around and buy different kinds of dried fruit for this. just tomatoes, etc! makes excellent dehydrated fruits and veg-etables; try flavors like carrots, bell peppers, and corn. mix with fruits like apricot, persimmons, or blackberries. portion out small amounts into reusable containers and store for a grab-and-go snack.

happy trails mix

makes 3½ cups

preparation * Combine all the ingredients and store in an airtight container or snack-size bags for up to 2 weeks. Use a permanent marker to write an expiration date on each bag. Keep one in the car for hunger emergencies.

recipe note

↘ Pine nuts are small, soft, and easy to chew for little mouths.

ingredients

½ cup shredded
unsweetened coconut
(see note)

2 cups rolled oats

1 cup coarsely
chopped pecans or
almonds

¼ cup flax meal
or wheat germ

¼ cup unsalted
sunflower seeds

1 tablespoon sesame
seeds or flax seeds

½ cup honey or
maple syrup

1 stick (½ cup)
butter, melted

1½ teaspoons
ground cinnamon

¼ teaspoon
ground nutmeg

¼ cup dried currants
or golden raisins

granola is easy to make and store, and it is perfect plain as a snack or on top of yogurt. add any kind of nut or dried fruit; blueberries or dried cranberries give it a flavorful punch.

grab-and-grow granola

makes about 4½ cups

preparation * Preheat the oven to 350°F.

Spread the coconut on a rimmed baking sheet and bake for about 3 to 4 minutes, or until the edges are golden brown. It can burn quickly, so keep an eye on it. Remove from the oven, transfer to a shallow dish and set aside.

Line a rimmed baking sheet with parchment paper and set aside.

In a large bowl, combine the oats, pecans, flax meal, sunflower seeds, and sesame seeds and set aside.

In a small bowl, stir together the honey, butter, cinnamon, and nutmeg. Pour the liquid over the oat mixture and stir well to combine. Spread the mixture on the

prepared baking sheet and bake for about 20 minutes, checking to make sure it is not burning. When the edges start to become slightly dark, remove from the oven and cool. Break up the granola with your hands or a spatula and add the coconut and currants. Store in an airtight container for up to 2 weeks.

recipe notes

↘ You can also add desiccated coconut to this for a snowier look.

↘ Omit raisins to keep the granola crispy.

↘ Large-flake unsweetened coconut is great to add to cookies for a chewy texture. Toast it for a crisper texture.

this is mildly sweet and very simple to make. it is less sugary than flavored yogurt, and the creamy white texture is balanced with the slight surprise of crunchy coconut. dip pretzels or fresh or dried fruit, or spread it on crackers.

ingredients

One 5.3-ounce container plain Greek-style yogurt (see note)

¼ cup sweetened flake coconut

1 teaspoon honey

1 teaspoon vanilla extract

creamy cloud dip

makes about 1¼ cups

preparation * Mix together the yogurt, coconut, honey, and vanilla in a bowl; chill, and serve.

recipe note

↘ For instructions on how to make thick-style yogurt, see page 127.

ingredients

1 cup crisp rice
cereal or Cheerios

½ cup nonfat dry milk

¼ cup creamy or
chunky peanut butter

¼ cup honey

¼ cup quick-cooking oats

this is a high-protein and fun snack for after school. these globs taste like a cookie but are full of peanut-y goodness. and it's a great way to use up those little amounts of cereal that are always left at the bottom of the box. mix all kinds together, trying different combinations of dry cereals. for a twist, serve these on a popsicle stick.

peanut butter globe globs

makes 12 balls

preparation * Crush the cereal in a zip-top bag using a mallet, and set aside.

Place the milk, peanut butter, honey, and oats and ½ cup of the crushed cereal in a bowl and mix well. Form the mixture into 1-inch balls. Add the balls to the bag with the remaining cereal. Shake and squeeze gently, coating them thoroughly with the mixture.

Serve immediately, or store in an airtight container in the refrigerator for 5 days or in the freezer indefinitely.

variations
↘ Roll the balls in coconut, cocoa powder, or crushed nuts or sesame seeds.

dips are fun and interactive for toddlers. they can scoop this one up with cut veggies and fruit or spread it onto slices of bread.

tropical glop

makes 1½ cups

preparation * Place the cream cheese in a microwave-safe bowl and heat on high for 20 seconds to soften. Add the fruit, carrots, and salt to the bowl, and use a stick blender to blend for 2 minutes, or until combined.

To toast the coconut, place it in a dry sauté pan on medium heat and watch closely. When you see it starting to turn light brown, stir the coconut around constantly to brown the rest evenly. Then pour it onto a plate to stop cooking.

Sprinkle the dip with the toasted coconut. Serve with apple slices or carrot, celery, or pretzel sticks.

toddler tip
Have your child "draw" shapes on their plate using the veggie as a pen and the dip as the ink.

ingredients

8 ounces cream cheese

One 8-ounce can crushed pineapple, drained

Two 4-ounce fruit cups, tropical or peach, drained

½ cup diced or shredded carrots

⅛ teaspoon kosher salt

½ cup toasted unsweetened desiccated coconut

string cheese is not usually a food we need to convince children to eat, but this is a fun way to enjoy it. it teaches kids about different textures, colors, and tastes—and they can double dip all they want! choose some of the dips from the list below, or create your own ideas.

double dippin' cheese sticks

makes 1 serving

choose four of the following ingredients

1 tablespoon white sesame seeds

1 tablespoon black sesame seeds

1 tablespoon poppy seeds

1 tablespoon applesauce

1 tablespoon crushed pine nuts, almonds, or peanuts

1 tablespoon crushed tortilla chips

1 tablespoon crushed crackers or goldfish crackers

1 piece string cheese

preparation * Put the dipping ingredients in separate small dishes on a plate with the cheese. Have your child dip the string cheese into each dish and discuss the different tastes. Take a bite and dip again.

* pantry-perfect shopping list *

↘ baked goods	↘ condiments	↘ snacks	↘ dry goods	↘ baking

↘ warehouse store	↘ deli	↘ rice and pasta	↘ canned	↘ beverages

↘ frozen	↘ fresh vegetables	↘ fresh fruit	↘ dairy	↘ meats
		↘ hygiene or drugstore		↘ miscellaneous

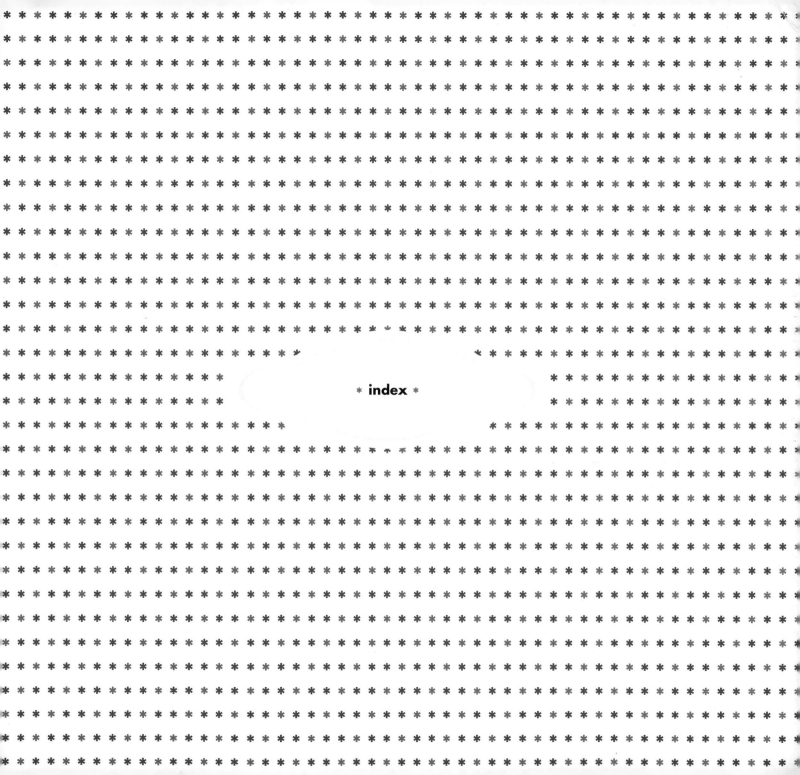

* index *

table of equivalents

the exact equivalents in the following tables have been rounded for convenience.

liquid/dry measurements

u.s.	metric
¼ teaspoon	1.25 milliliters
½ teaspoon	2.5 milliliters
1 teaspoon	5 milliliters
1 tablespoon (3 teaspoons)	15 milliliters
1 fluid ounce (2 tablespoons)	30 milliliters
¼ cup	60 milliliters
⅓ cup	80 milliliters
½ cup	120 milliliters
1 cup	240 milliliters
1 pint (2 cups)	480 milliliters
1 quart (4 cups, 32 ounces)	960 milliliters
1 gallon (4 quarts)	3.84 liters
1 ounce (by weight)	28 grams
1 pound	448 grams
2.2 pounds	1 kilogram

lengths

u.s.	metric
⅛ inch	3 millimeters
¼ inch	6 millimeters
½ inch	12 millimeters
1 inch	2.5 centimeters

oven temperature

fahrenheit	celsius	gas	fahrenheit	celsius	gas
250	120	½	400	200	6
275	140	1	425	220	7
300	150	2	450	230	8
325	160	3	475	240	9
350	180	4	500	260	10
375	190	5			